Finding Hope and Healing in Houston

J Spence

Introduction

J ust like a music composer, all the notes and keys for my book have been coalescing in my head for the last two years, but I have been unable to put the words on paper, simply because nobody knew how my story was going to end, and a composer cannot begin a symphony without the final act. When I received the news that I was officially in remission, feeling like a recharged battery, the memories of all the kind acts from people who cared and prayed for me reminded me that I owed them a book. I have written this book in my own words and shared it openly with authenticity. I do not wish this book to be anything grandiose but hope it will be impactful to anyone who reads it.

This book has been written in an irreverent form in the hope that, by being able to laugh at some of the events, it provides inspiration for others fighting for their lives as it did for me. I also want to share this book with all my loved ones who have been eagerly anticipating my ponderings on paper. From my point of view, writing this book is also a form of healing and self-therapy, as most patients know that cancer is often fought twice – once during treatment and a second time during recovery.

This book is not written as a cancer book because cancer books can be demoralizing. I also opted to write this book chronologically but supplemented it with some, hopefully useful, anecdotes that I learned during my adventure. If the reader detects any hints of self-pity in these chapters, it is only meant to demonstrate that this "cancer adventure" was like the symphony mentioned earlier. It has high and low notes. These low notes are in the book in order to not marginalize the severity of cancer. With the high notes, I want to share how I animate my life with gusto and bravery during and after treatment, and not with the intention of minimizing the evil that is cancer.

Enjoy the ride!

Dedication

This book is dedicated to my mother, who endured abandonment by her parents, the Second World War, and the trauma of Communist China. My mother's ability to embrace change, her unconditional love for me, and her bravery have sustained me over and over – not only in this journey but throughout my life.

I also want to thank our great friend, John R, who encouraged me to seek a second opinion for my cancer treatment – a true turning point to reverse a mistake. I am even more grateful I listened to his encouragement to write this book.

This book is also dedicated to my long-time buddy in life, Keith, who loves me with or without cancer. I am privileged to have a husband who educates me on how to utilize the English language to achieve greater clarification for my brainwaves in writing. He loves me at my best and my worst!

Acknowledgment

I am forever grateful to my lead oncologist, Dr. Westin, without whose fastidious attention to her patient's needs I would not have been able to sail through my cancer adventure. Also, to Dr. Klopp, a very special warm hug to you and your whole radiation team. You and your confidence carried me through my distress and elation.

There are family, friends, and strangers who all lived my illness daily and kept me encouraged. I will never forget the fellowship from these people who showered me with love and prayers. The impact of an act of kindness or a positive comment from a stranger half a world away cannot be dismissed, and with my daughter's positive attitude and my husband's boundless patience, I survived and won!

Author's Notes

The names of my husband, daughter, and my siblings and public figures are real, but other personal names are disguised. Specific permission was obtained to use some of the doctors' real names.

MD Anderson is a part of University of Texas but for simplicity, the institution's name has been shortened to MD Anderson.

Contents

Chapter One

My Daughter's Hello Kitty Socks

"God whispers to us in our pleasures, speaks in our conscience, but shouts in our pains: It is His megaphone to rouse a deaf world." – C. S. Lewis

It was April 2, 2021, a beautiful and sunny morning in Chicago. I was just another multi-tasking, motivated mother and IT consultant working on a large client project. It is often said in research that women tend to easily manage more than one task at a time, and that was (emphasis on the *was*) definitely my trademark.

I woke up very early to lead some conference calls with my colleagues in Brazil and Mexico, feeling energized and full of anticipation for a great day at work (from home due to the COVID-19 pandemic). Since I had a full day overflowing with meetings, I decided to brush my teeth while I was on a conference call.

As I was brushing my teeth at the sink, pain radiated from my right calf. The pain was so intense, it was like being attacked by a knife-wielding robber piercing my vein. I dropped my toothbrush and fell to the ground. The pain persisted, and I still decided to stand up to attend my conference calls. My commitment to my work had always been indisputable, but it was a Friday, and I was looking forward to the weekend where my beloved husband, Keith, and I had our thirty-fourth wedding anniversary to celebrate.

As the day went by, the pain didn't go away. Keith and my daughter, Gigi, were somewhat troubled by this sudden condition. They could see I was in pain, but I still insisted on attending to work. The dedicated part of my brain told me the pain was likely not serious. Perhaps I slept awkwardly and jammed my leg muscles, or I injured my muscles on the treadmill the previous day – certainly not anything to be unduly alarmed by.

Being resourceful and determined, I pulled out a pair of my husband's old compression socks and struggled with his old tight sock on my right leg. I proceeded to lead my work calls without a break. I worked a full day standing up next to my laptop not realizing the horrors that were about to unfold.

On the morning of the fourth of April, having slept with the compression sock all night, I needed to release myself from it. As I took the sock off, the agony was beyond words. So, my husband insisted that I give my doctor a call. My doctor urged me to check in at my local hospital for further investigation.

It was our thirty-fourth wedding anniversary. I was not pleased to spend the day at the hospital. Reluctantly, I complied and drove myself with my husband to our local hospital to ease my family's concerns.

As I lay on the emergency room (ER) gurney irritated but eager to go home to celebrate our wedding anniversary, a young ER doctor approached and stated that the team suspected that I might have a blood clot in my right calf. He didn't really believe that was the case, but to be safe, he ordered an investigative ultrasound scan - just to rule out any blood disorders.

A few hours later, the young doctor returned with a look of shock on his face and explained that I indeed did have a blood clot in my right calf. The proper medical diagnosis was an infrapopliteal venous thrombosis involving the mid and distal peroneal veins. My blood test also showed an elevated calcium serum. According to the standard operating procedure, I was to be prescribed some blood thinners immediately before I was allowed to return home. I was discharged from the ER, just in time to begin our Easter Sunday egg hunt at home.

I remember Keith and Gigi walking around our property for Easter eggs. I followed behind the two of them, snatching some photographs and videos, thinking to myself how sweet and content my life was, having these two rascals in my world. The father-and-daughter bond between my husband and daughter often reminded me how close I was to my father.

Gigi had just had one of her hip surgeries to cure her hip dysplasia. With the effects of the surgery, Gigi was not mobile, but she was determined to move around using her orthopedic crutches. She was clonking around the property eagerly collecting these Easter eggs before her father could lay his hands on them. Keith was the one who made up the Easter eggs with clues and hints for Gigi, pretending he did not know where the eggs were hidden. Although those eggs never had her name on them, her competitiveness led to her desire to win against her father. It was quite amusing to watch them fighting over Easter treats. I suspect my daughter's fighting spirit and determination stemmed from my DNA.

As I administered the blood thinner medicine as prescribed, on April 14, 2021, I developed postmenopausal bleeding. A quick call to my doctor led to an immediate referral to my gynecologist. I underwent a vaginal ultrasound at the gynecologist's office. The technician was able to detect a mass from the scan.

The oncologist's physician's assistant (PA) placed me in a pelvic checkup position, i.e., legs apart and facing the lackluster ceiling of a doctor's office. I distinctly remembered staring at my lovely pair of Hello Kitty socks, which I borrowed from my daughter, with my legs spread wide like a mother in labor, all kinds of dark thoughts clouding my head. I was somewhat embarrassed when my socks were exposed. I smiled at my socks and explained to the PA that I left my house in a hurry and pulled out my daughter's socks by mistake. Looking back, I lived such a hectic life I was a constant sock-stealer in my family.

As the PA started to gather some biopsy samples from my cervix, I distinctly remembered I was curating my words as to how I was going to tell my beloved husband, who had to wait in his car due to the COVID-19 restriction. I held back my tears as I looked at lumps and lumps of ugly samples that the PA was collecting. The whole biopsy process was visible to me as I lay on the leg-wide-apart child-bearing position. The collected samples were stored in a translucent plastic container right in front of my eyes. I could see the samples collected resembled fermented and raw hamburger meat, lifeless and extremely obnoxious but bloody. As the doctor's assistant shook her head and told me this was "bad," my heart sank, and I knew the biopsy would bring some unpleasant news.

It seemed that the biopsy process took a long time. As the PA left the examination room, she told me to hold on while she consulted with a doctor in the office. I remembered staring at my daughter's Hello Kitty socks and wondering how my life was going to change from that moment onwards. Inevitably, I orchestrated the words in my head so I would not shock my husband.

Within a swift moment, another female doctor entered the room. She introduced herself. She proceeded to point to her wall chart of what a female reproductive system consisted of. I felt like I was back in high school for a lesson in biology. Being an irascible patient, I asked the doctor if I had a cancerous tumor.

The PA and doctor looked at each other, and the doctor said that the medical team needed to have a biopsy result before she could conclude it was malignant. Both the PA and doctor left the room whispering to each other. I was sure they were comparing notes about my tumor, not wanting to discuss it in front of me.

The PA returned and assisted me in getting out of bed. She was very sympathetic and whispered in my ears, "This is serious, and I want you to seek immediate medical treatment."

As I was dressing, all I could remember was my daughter's Hello Kitty socks on my feet. The rest was a blur. I walked back to my husband, who had already texted me four times while I was being examined. Tears began to well up in my eyes, and I was shaking like a leaf in an autumn wind.

I got in the car, and I did not break down. As I was delivering my carefully curated words, I noticed my voice was somewhat shaky, as if I had been hit by lightning. The vaginal cervical biopsy was an invasive experience, but the anticipated outcome cast a gloomy shadow over me. I was in the prime of my life, enjoying a very successful career before the blood clot incident. I was not ready to confront a deadly disease called cancer.

Keith and I both knew our life had just been transformed, and this was uncharted territory on the battlefield of cancer!

Chapter Two

Receiving and Processing My Diagnosis

*"C*ancer is a word, not a sentence." *– Unknown.*

Following the cervical biopsy, my oncologist's office ordered a computer tomography (CT) scan of the abdomen and pelvis on April 16. The CT showed a lobular hypodense adjacent to the right posterior of the uterus, and the mass expanded into the lower pelvis. The mass appeared to be strongly attached to my rectum. This was not a good sign. On April 19, a magnetic resonance imaging (MRI) was ordered, which showed a large, complex, solid tumor posteriorly from the uterus, and at this point of the investigation, an ovarian-originated cancer could not be ruled out.

As soon as the results from the biopsy, CT, and MRI were available, I met with the head of the gynecology team. I distinctly remember it was another beautiful April morning, and I had to leave Keith behind, sitting in his car waiting for me. The extra stress of the COVID-19 constraints did not help my situation. Having to see the gynecologist alone was an unpleasant experience and one that I wouldn't want anyone to encounter. Being alone with no support system or just a pair of arms to hug me was difficult, notwithstanding that I had nobody to help me understand and process all the medical jargon I was about to receive.

I had steeled myself for the worst news. I began to take stock of my life as I waited, for what seemed an interminable time, for the formal declaration of my fate, and I reflected on the lifeless and soulless white room with no personality in which I found myself waiting. Those white, fluorescent ceiling lights of the doctor's office were never meant to inspire anyone as I paced up and down the tiny ten by ten patient room.

Finally, the head of the medical team entered the room. I was immediately concerned when it appeared he was sweating and more nervous than me. I did notice that he was very neatly dressed in a white shirt that must have been starched and his hair was extremely glossy with hair wax. Then, I momentarily felt like a defendant in a courtroom waiting for the verdict from the judge.

The doctor had entered the room with a gentle knock on the door, as if he did not want to startle me. He introduced himself and then began elucidating how female reproductive organs were structured. He was puzzled by the fact that I did not have any period for twenty-three years and felt that should have been a red flag. It seemed like I was sitting in Mr. Koh's – my high school biology teacher – class learning about puberty again.

Cautiously, with much deliberation and thoughtfulness, the doctor explained to me that I had an advanced-stage endometrial cancer that was beyond his expertise, and hence, it was appropriate for him to pass me to a local gynecological oncologist. His shimmering waxy dark hair was decorated with sweat as he was not sure how I would react to his verdict. I saw blood gradually leaving his face as he delivered my potential death sentence.

"Has any doctor carried out a pelvic examination during your yearly wellness checkup?" the doctor asked me.

"No," I responded.

The doctor shook his head and said, "I do not know how long this large tumor has been around, but a yearly checkup should have detected it. We urgently need to get some input from an oncologist."

As I heard his words, the dictionary in my brain swiftly correlated the word *oncologist* with *cancer*. I had already processed the initial diagnosis, so at that point I could be objective in assessing what I had heard, and the outlook on my health had migrated to another level of fear. I remained without emotion, thinking it would help to calm the doctor. Instead of being bowed down by grief and wrapping myself in self-pity, I wanted to tell this doctor it was not his fault that I had cancer. I felt sorry for any individual who had to deliver a cancer diagnosis to a patient, but this guy's mouth was as wide as a guppy fish during feeding time and looking like he needed more oxygen, and the sweat running down his greased-up hair could not escape my observant eyes. In some comforting way, I have to admit, I felt like this doctor needed a warm hug more than I did.

From that appointment on, there was no ambiguity as to what disease I had, and my health was not in a good place. Mentally, I was still strong, but my physical well-being became weak very quickly such that I could barely walk two steps from my parked car to the curb. The tumor seemed to be growing as fast as a wild mushroom after a spring rain. Toby – I will explain later the genesis of that name – could not destroy my hope or my spirit, but it did begin to cripple my body. My head began to hum the song that went like, "If I die young, bury me in satin..."

It was also fascinating to me that it seemed that humans' brains are designed to process bad news faster than good news. In my case, my brain rapidly switched into action mode. I wanted to seek medical help from an oncologist before I left the gynecologist's office. I felt I was too young to die, but at the same time began to set priorities, and the top of that list was to try and prolong my life so I might at least be present at Gigi's college graduation about a year later.

Chapter Three

First Instinct Was Not Always the Right Instinct

"*Wearing stoma bags can be draining.*" – *Unknown*

Armed with the scientific data of my disease, I sought an immediate appointment with a local well-known surgeon who specialized in gynecological cancer. I liked the surgeon immensely. He gave me his undivided attention and excellent bedside manner. His medical training not only gave him some good surgical skills, but he also came well-heeled with patient-centric consulting skills and demonstrated great sensitivity.

That time, in spite of COVID-19, the doctor allowed my husband to be in the room provided we all wore masks and observed the appropriate safety protocols. With my husband holding my right hand, receiving the words from the surgeon was a bitter pill sweetened ever so slightly.

The surgeon carefully assessed my tumor via vaginal and rectum examination and concluded that the tumor had grown substantially to the size of a grapefruit. It was firmly attached and had distorted my rectum. Further enlargement would soon have impacts on other nearby vital organs with the physiological impression on my liver, kidneys, pancreas, and gallbladder. At that point, I was not in an immense amount of pain, but I was losing a substantial amount of weight as the days went by.

Given the tumor had grown from 4.1 cm to 8.1 cm over ten days, there was no time to procrastinate. I asked the surgeon what options were available to prolong my life and was told that probably the safest course of action was immediate surgery to debulk the pelvic area. This would be the normal option in a case such as mine. However, the outcome of such a radical surgery would mean I would have to forgo my bodily functions for urination and waste discharge. This meant wearing two ostomy bags for the rest of my life.

The alternative option was to begin aggressive chemotherapy for two to three years but with no guarantee that the tumor could be eviscerated. The word *chemotherapy* cast such a dark shadow in my head, which reminded me how my beloved brother Richard went through only three chemotherapy infusions and how he had suffered a painful death within five months of his diagnosis. My doubts about chemotherapy as a treatment option against my cancer did not predispose me to select that option either.

Given the limited choices, I asked the surgeon for two things. The first was the ability to attend my daughter's graduation in May 2022. The second was to repair me sufficiently so I would be well enough to travel to Singapore because I wanted to share my news with my mother. The surgeon looked me in the eyes and told me he would try his very best and swiftly handed me a full box of Kleenex.

My future appeared to be pretty dismal. I vaguely remember that my eyes were cloudy for the rest of the consultation with the surgeon, and the room began to become a blur with sadness. My mind started to wonder how I could wear a nice dress to my daughter's graduation with the embellishment of two stoma bags. More importantly, how would my brothers and sisters bear the burden of telling my mother that her youngest daughter might leave the building without bidding farewell?

Having committed to the upfront surgical management, the surgeon recommended an inferior vena cava (IVC) filter to be implanted to prevent further episodes of pulmonary embolism. The IVC was proposed to prevent any heart attacks or strokes. The cancer confronting me did have a tendency to fabricate random blood clots. Radical hysterectomy surgery might also carry a high risk of blood clots. The implant of the IVC filter took place very swiftly in preparation for the surgery, which was planned for one week after my second dose of the COVID-19 vaccination. The oncologist surgeon did not want to operate when I had too recently had my second COVID-19 vaccine.

Keith and I went home blessed with one week to plan out the surgery. At that point, we had no inclination to seek a second opinion. I was slowly embracing my fate of wearing two bags for the rest of my life in order to save it. I even spent a few hours googling the best-looking ostomy bags available. Some had flowers printed, some had fake Gucci patterns, and some even had plain skin colors to make them less invasive. I was beginning to embrace my new way of surviving. I also watched a few YouTube videos to learn how stoma bags were used and disposed of.

In an attempt to cheer me up, Gigi said that, on the bright side, I would never have to visit a bacteria-infested public toilet on the plane when we traveled. Somehow, her analogy and optimistic viewpoint were on point. Who wants to use a public toilet during the peak of COVID-19? Perhaps my family was trying to put on a brave face by being upbeat, or they were merely hiding their anxiety. I may never find out.

Somehow, in the winds of change, I found my true calling. As my disease got worse each day, I had to transition my clients and stop working so I could focus on my encounter with this despicable tumor. Alas, no more was I to fly through my days at two hundred miles per hour; I was to slow everything down and truly rest my body. It caused me to reflect on if I slowed down enough and listened to my daughter when she tried to get my attention. I was chasing large profits in my business and sometimes forgot to pause to take a look at the view or consider people who longed to have a moment of my time. I started to question whether I had run out of time to practice my role as a mother. Would someone above me give me a do-over? I was a good provider financially, but I forgot how my daughter had grown up while I was dashing through my work life. Would this mother do-over be curtailed by my illness?

Being intertwined with a hard-to-cure disease was the wake-up call I needed. I realized my life was, perhaps, out of focus for many years, and I was hurrying through my life instead of savoring the blessings I was granted. I almost missed attending my daughter's graduation or bidding farewell to my elderly mother. I was not proud of myself when I became a burden to my husband with this current predicament. To quote Keith, I was not completely lost, but I was temporarily unsure of my position after receiving such a prognosis. I began to realize life could be fleeting and frail.

Chapter Four

Option of
an Exemplary
U-Turn

"For every complex problem there is an answer that is clear, simple, and wrong!"- H.L. Mencken

While Keith and I were planning and mapping my fate, and patiently waiting for my upcoming surgery, we thought of consulting a good friend of ours, Mr. John R, who had made an excellent recommendation for Gigi's hip surgery. It seemed that both Keith and I were not ready to accept surgery as the only way to deal with my tumor. Keith wondered whether our friend would have any doctors he would recommend.

Within five minutes of talking to John R, we received a phone call back from him that we must make an appointment with either University of Texas MD Anderson Cancer Center in Houston, Texas, or Memorial Sloane Kettering Cancer Center in New York, given Gigi was studying at Columbia University in New York. John R strongly encouraged us not to accept surgery as the only approach to eliminate my tumor. He believed that all medical treatment recommendations need to undergo due diligence, and we had nothing to lose by contacting another provider. Obtaining a second opinion during our waiting period could cause no harm or delay the surgery.

Looking back, taking John R's advice was the best decision I've made in my entire life.

John R gave Keith very specific action items and instructions to connect with MD Anderson. We both acted on the instructions and secured the very first oncologist appointment with MD Anderson.

John R's family are kind and genuine friends who would share our limousine or ride in a bus with us when the limousine was broken. John R and his wife, Susan, have three children, two girls and a boy. The two girls are die-hard equestrians like their mother. One of their daughters was a team member of my daughter when they competed at the Kentucky Horse Park for the pony finals in the Jumper division.

I always had very fond memories of John R's private golf cart, which was decked out with a full bar. When John R made a cocktail, the size of the pour was always generous. During the pony finals, Keith and John R were tasked with taking videos of our girls' jumping rounds. Somehow, many of those videos did not exist, or, if they existed, the videos appeared to have been filmed by a couple of raccoons on weed. Under the influence of John R's cocktails, the video footage mainly captured the sand on the arena and was not quite what Susan and I had wished for. Nonetheless, a jolly good time was had. One could always trust John R's family to throw a good party at the horse shows.

At the various shows, John R was often the culprit who relaxed Keith so much that they both could not remember the primary purpose of the competition. One summer, we met with the John R family at their private trailer decked out like a bar in Manhattan. Not only was there a large selection of liquors, but the trailer was also embellished with neon lights and came complete with a licensed bartender. Given we all trusted John R's cocktail skills, and that Keith had virtually put his life in John R's hands at all the horse shows, what was there to prevent us from listening to his advice on seeking the right doctors?

Based on John R's advice, Keith and I caught the very first flight to Houston and were on our way to the Mecca of the cancer center, MD Anderson, the very next day. Before we knew it, the plane emerged from the gunmetal overcast and landed with barely a bump at Houston Airport.

Keith and I often looked back and described our decision to pause the surgery and fly down to Houston in the nick of time was the equivalent to missing a flight that crashed. I was on an inexorable march to life-changing surgery, but I was lucky enough to have John R as a friend and was twice as lucky to have the common sense to seek his input. In hindsight, to proceed with the surgery would have been a poor decision. Getting a second opinion about my cancer treatment was the mother of all luck. The amount of gratitude towards the John R family could never be marginalized, and I knew that, apart from the doctors, John R genuinely gave me a new lease on life. He threw me a floating wood door just like Jack Dawson to Rose in *Titanic*!

Chapter Five

New Chemical Warfare Strategy

"We must be willing to pay a price for freedom." – H.L. Mencken

Life had taken me to an unlikely place not congruent with my roadmap for life – MD Anderson at Houston Medical Center. I will never forget my first impression of the massive medical facilities. The whole place was overwhelming but state-of-the-art. I could only relate my excitement at seeing MD Anderson to my very first experience at Disneyworld.

That first visit to the MD Anderson facilities was during the peak of the COVID-19 pandemic. The strict rules only allowed patients to enter the buildings without a family escort. However, I did not complain and said to myself, "That's life! Pull yourself together and get on with it!" Fate sometimes puts out a foot to trip you, but I told myself that I should accept that I was extraordinarily lucky to be treated at the best cancer care institute, and if COVID-19 threw a few roadblocks, I would just deal with it and march into the hospital alone. I kissed Keith goodbye and followed the yellow brick road just like Dorothy.

Meeting my oncologist, Dr. Westin, was an uplifting experience. Dr. Westin had very long and curly hair. Her intelligence shined right through her intellectual spectacles, but most of all, she listened. She listened with all her focus and demonstrated remarkably how she knew what my needs were. Dr. Westin did an initial assessment of my condition, and she did not appear to be overly daunted by the size of the tumor given that she had treated thousands of cancer patients. She was, however, concerned as to where the tumor resided.

With great confidence, Dr. Westin informed me that surgery was not the only way to fight Toby – I hated the word *cancer* and hence had chosen the name Toby for this recalcitrant tumor. I was somewhat surprised; for a surgeon not to opt for a surgical procedure was surprising. Meeting Dr. Westin was like a breath of fresh air, and she gave me the indisputable impression that she had dealt with my kind of cancer many times before. I was definitely inspired! It was a complete paradigm shift, and I began to feel hopeful and that the stars at night indeed were brighter deep in the heart of Texas.

Dr. Westin explained how the cancer board review process worked at MD Anderson. It was comforting that no treatment plan could proceed unless verified and approved by a panel of experts as part of the due diligence process. My lead oncologist, Dr. Westin, would have to propose a treatment plan in front of MD Anderson's weekly cancer board before we could commence any treatment.

The cancer board deliberated, and the recommendation was to begin a series of neoadjuvant chemotherapy infusions, consisting of two platinum-based agents of Carboplatin and Paclitaxel. Neoadjuvant chemotherapy means that chemotherapy takes place before the main treatment, such as surgery. An army of nurses and PAs would march into the patient's room to provide some guidance on what to expect from platinum-based chemotherapy. The likelihood of hair loss was high, and I was provided with options for a cold cap device to attempt to preserve my long hair. Losing my hair from cancer could have been traumatic, but I convinced myself that my hair did not define me because real beauty emanates from within. I decided to let my hair go!

Meanwhile, Keith and I decided that since life is about to be interrupted, we may as well leave our beautiful home and move to a corporate apartment in Houston, at least temporarily. There is no doubt this was a good – but expensive – call. My body would have been too weak to handle commuting coupled with the frequent risk of COVID-19 exposure. A ship in the harbor is safe, but my ship could no longer be hiding out in my cozy home if my cancer was to be dealt with properly.

It began to dawn on me why my mother-in-law used to compare life to British bakery goods - that a perfect English crumpet needed to be full of holes to be light and lofty to allow for butter to melt in. The holes in my crumpet were leaving my beloved horses, cats, and daughter behind. And so it goes, what do you do when life gives you lemons except...make lemon tarts? I also believed that every storm has a developing stage – that I was experiencing – and a mature stage – still to come – but eventually there would be the dissipating stage, which would provide safe harbor again. I also learned that, courtesy of social media, the whole world had an opinion about how to handle my cancer. But I quickly learned the lesson of the day: seek out the best possible experts in the field, experts whose reputations had been built over decades of research and successful treatments, innovation, and statistically proven results. Also, a second medical opinion could make a colossal difference to the outcome and my well-being.

Chapter Six

All Rivers Flow into the Same Sea

"*Suffering is a characteristic of life. You can't take it personally.*"
    – *Unknown*

Every story has an end, but in a cancer patient's life, every ending is just a new chapter. This was the closing of my prior chapter of a chemo-free body. At that point in my life, I did not wish to hear the best was behind but that the worst was yet to come. My emotions were complex and tough to explain. Despite the odds, I believed there was a chance that I could still offer something meaningful to my family and loved ones.

Upon arriving at the reception of MD Anderson with Keith for my first chemotherapy infusion, I was praying that, after following protocol and the Q&A for COVID-19 clearance, Keith would be allowed to accompany me. The security guard asked me why I needed to be accompanied. I said it was because I was petrified for my first chemotherapy. The security guard very firmly replied, "That is not a good reason."

With that said, Keith was not allowed to enter the building with me. I was brave and did not feel abandoned, but I did hear my inner voice humming the John Miles song, "All by myself! Don't wanna be, all by myself anymore!"

Keith wobbled his lips, but that did not work with the security guard.

Hearing I was just about to embark on chemotherapy, my girl-friend, Dr. Rhianna, had mailed me some crystals and rocks with a book. Out of all the rocks she gifted me, the purple crystal caught my eye, and it became my constant companion and good-luck charm. This purple rock was with me during every single infusion since it brought me so much calmness. Words from Dr. Rhianna, – "to give when we are strong; to receive when we need strength" – reverberated in my head as I sat in the waiting room for my infusion.

Sitting in the chemotherapy waiting room was an eye-opener for me. It became evident that cancer is not prejudiced because it did not discriminate against age, race, gender, religion, or color of skin. What was most heartbreaking though was to see young adults in this sea of patients. That gave me a reality check, and I soon realized I was somewhat blessed to be alive and having lived healthily for fifty-eight years. My daily walk from the apartment to my cancer treatment also involved passing the large children's hospital packed full of very young patients who were more courageous than me. I saw these weakened children and realized hope for a cancer cure was like Houston's sun-shine behind the tall children's hospital building. The sun may cast a shadow of sadness frequently, but it also can give inspiration when you step out into the light.

As I played with my silky long hair, I realized my look was soon to change - from Rapunzel to Lord Voldemort overnight by the poiso-nous platinum chemicals in my veins. These chemicals were meant to kill everything but me. Doing what was right – even though it would be grueling – was my weapon to begin my battle with Toby. Chemotherapy was never on my holiday wish list, but to be afraid and having to march forward with this life-changing experience was a reality I had to confront.

Throughout my treatment, I repudiated letting anyone in my family enter the cancer center with me, conveniently imposed by the strict COVID-19 stipulation. Where revenge is a dish best served cold, I believed chemotherapy is a cocktail best served unaccompanied. I sat patiently in the waiting room, feeling so lonesome among an ocean of cancer comrades. Some people looked pale, frail, and near death. Some patients were staring at the ceiling, looking like they had relinquished their lives and left the building mentally, but I came to realize it was just because chemo is difficult. The pale faces with vacant expressions from my comrades led me to wonder if Jesus still dwelled in Houston. In three words, I summed up all I had learned from life: life is hard!

In an unspoken manner, I understood that all cancer patients are connected like rivers, and all rivers should eventually flow into the same sea. The sea of cancer patients would have waves and storms. Some patients were traveling in their small kayaks, and some were in the cruise liners. No matter what vessels we were in, we were all in the same storm. Someone once said, "A river trembles with fear before entering the sea," and I was that quivering river in anticipation of the big body of water. That sea was so incalculable, and that river – me – had no real option to go back. I feared I would disappear and become just another number in the cancer ocean. In this ocean of cancer, the tides could roll in gradually with gentle waves one day. On others, the tide could come thundering and crush one's spirit.

I began to seek a lifeboat. I gazed around the infusion waiting room, and all I could see was sorrowful fellow cancer warriors with the customary baldness and an uncomprehending expression, or hairless heads disguised with hats or wigs. I began to wonder how I got myself into this not-so-exclusive club of cancer.

I saw a pale-looking lady who could barely stand up holding on to her husband, clearly traveling in a tiny and sinking kayak in the cancer ocean. After a while, the lady could stand no more and crumpled to the floor. The sound of her falling would always be seared in my head, and I was not even related to that patient. I wonder what it would be like for the patient's loved ones to witness the fall.

It saddened me to be alone for my very first infusion, but it would have been harder for my husband to witness this sea of sickness. I had always maintained that chemotherapy experiences were best endured alone rather than sharing with one's partner. From that day onwards, I became determined and never permitted my husband or my sister to come with me. Keith and my sister often begged to accompany me, but I never relented. Caregivers of cancer patients are often much more tormented than the patients; they are able to see the suffering, and yet they feel stranded and helpless.

After adequate, but satisfactory blood work, my oncologist gave me her medical clearance to proceed with my very first chemotherapy. I was in some way wishing it was not going to go ahead, but I knew it was the necessary treatment in my situation. As I was connected to various intravenous (IV) lines, I positioned myself flat on the hospital bed, staring into the soulless white ceiling of the treatment room. Losing my illusion of being wholesome and organic, I reflected that if I was a chicken on an organic farm, why would I voluntarily be injected with the most poisonous chemicals in my veins? How would a rational person react to knowing the amount of medical expenses my insurance company had to pay so that I could be poisoned over an eight-hour infusion? The idea of being poisoned so I might heal was incompatible with my logical mind. If that was the paradise of cancer cure, what would the abyss for patients without the chance to be treated look like?

As I stared at coconut trees painted on the ceiling tiles, tears started to flow, smudging my finely drawn mascara eyes. I wanted to cry, but my makeup looked so good right at that moment. I had carefully curated my perfect wings which were on point to stop me from tearing up, but I failed. Hopefully nobody saw me looking like a raccoon after a food fight because I was all alone.

I felt so lonely that I started to cry for my mom like a newborn baby needing warm hugs from her breastfeeding mother. That was the first time in my life that I wished to return to my mother's womb. Given all the tubes in me, when tears started to flood my ears, I told myself that there was no one here to dry my ears because I needed to be the captain of this journey! That was when I pulled myself together and told myself that fight or flight was not a choice, and it would take a lot of bravery to stand up to Toby.

Perhaps I was being melodramatic, but I did imagine getting my first chemotherapy was equivalent to a person on death row drawing their last breath after lethal injection. I began to petition my inner self for companionship. This inner voice was co-habiting in my head, and it talked to me when I was nervous. The voice asked me whether it should unplug me and let me escape. As my inner self was braver than the real me, it started to remind me how important it was to get medical treatment if I ever wanted to see my daughter's graduation ceremony or visit my elderly mother again.

After my inner self became quiet, I kicked into a state where I referred to myself as a third person. In this involuntary reflex, I removed myself from the unavoidable chemotherapy. The voice I heard said, "Josephine, don't be afraid. Stay still and let Jesus take the wheel!" That was my way to unencumber my mind from my physical body as if "Josephine" was just a third person hovering over me for support and to cheer me on. In a very peculiar way, I became an observer of my own thoughts.

I decided that escaping chemotherapy at this juncture would be cowardly. My mind started to play back to my carefree days when I was a young kid. The coconut trees on the decorative ceiling tiles reminded me of my hometown in tropical Malaysia where there is an abundance of them. The images which came to my head were my untroubled playtime with my brothers and sisters, eating my mother's homecooked meals, and sitting on my father's lap telling him what I wanted to be when I grew up. Among all these thoughts, my inner self returned to trouble me, and my biggest apprehension was how I was supposed to tell my mother about my cancer. After all, my mother had lost her second newborn baby and her fourth son, and no parent should have to experience burying their children more than once.

When the nurses entered the infusion room, my inner self dissipated, and I no longer felt mentally alone. The nurses were very sympathetic. They took the time to explain, with compassion, how the chemotherapy process would work. First, the cocktail of chemicals was "cooked" near the infusion room called "the hood" because the pharmacists actually did "cook" the chemical agents in a secure kitchen with a hood. The proportion of the chemicals was calculated based on my weight and height, i.e., the Body Mass Index (BMI).

When the cocktail was ready, the infusion nurses would double and triple-check the label on the medication against the patient's name badge. No infusion could commence until at least three independent people had verified that the correct medication, in all respects, was being used. The three independent individuals were the infusion nurse, the patient, and another nurse on the team. Care was essential to avoid any mistakes.

Once the verification had been completed, the infusion nurse would start the pre-chemotherapy drugs. First, there was the initial flushing of the IV with saline followed by the sedative antihistamine: Benadryl. When the Benadryl was main-lined into the veins, my reactions were a combination of leg-shaking and drunkenness. Strange as it might seem, I had the urge to sing in a foreign language when antihistamines were streaming in my veins. Nobody can explain it.

As the first chemotherapy drug, Paclitaxel, registered in my veins, there was a strange, warming sensation in my arms. As the chemicals flowed through, a peculiar metallic taste appeared on my tongue. It was an alien and unique buzz on the right side of my body. The experience was not particularly arduous but merely odd. It was never clear to me why some chemotherapy drugs caused this metallic taste, but the nurses did advise me to buy some top-quality plastic utensils should the metallic taste remain.

The second chemotherapy drug, Carboplatin, swiftly followed. In a very idiosyncratic way, I was able to taste a different flavor on my tongue. This time my tongue did not perceive a metallic sensation; instead, it was like a tingling numbness around the mouth.

When all the prescribed medicines had been infused, the wrap-up was some flushing of saline solution as a cleansing agent to avoid infection. In the meantime, the nurses offered me a large tub of ice to desensitize the unorthodox tastes in my mouth. I guess that was the beginning of how my taste buds were altered, and it explains a lot of the reasons why I started to have aversion to certain foods.

I was a pale person on blood thinners, so the vein used for the infusion became somewhat bruised. The colorful rainbow on my arms began to look like I had gone a couple of rounds with Muhammad Ali. As I was a new chemotherapy patient, I was not aware there was an option to have a port implanted under my chest skin to avoid damage to my veins. Looking back, it would have been very beneficial to begin with a chemotherapy device for infusion.

I remember sharing a photo of my bruised arms with my colleague. He yelled at me in his thick Italian accent, "Guuurll! Are you sure you went to a doctor and not a vampire?"

These multi-layered colors of green, blue, dark purple, and yellow on my arms reminded me of my childhood dessert from Malaysia called *Kueh-Lapis*. Funny how people's minds wander back to their childhood memories when they are fighting to survive!

After the first infusion, I did not lose my identity; instead, I joined this big chemotherapy ocean that transformed me into a mighty combatant. Admittedly, I was looking for a fast car to escape my first chemotherapy, but once I overcame the initial reluctance and foot-dragging, I acknowledged the cards that I had been dealt. I realized cancer is a word and not an outcome. The death-row-like feelings began to dissipate, and the voice in my head began to quiet. I did still wonder why the poisonous infusion was given the name "chemotherapy" since the whole experience didn't feel therapeutic.

Chapter Seven

Braved the Shave

"*Women's liberation will not be achieved until a woman can become paunchy and bald, and still think she's attractive to the opposite sex.*" – Earl Wilson

The schedule of chemotherapy was one day of infusion followed by three weeks of recuperation. After my very first infusion, I was feeling great and was allowed to fly home just to catch a glimpse of the blossoming spring flowers in my backyard and visit the various animals. Balancing home life and cancer treatment was somewhat taxing when my chosen treatment center was one thousand two hundred miles away.

Although my hair did not fall out immediately after my first chemotherapy, I noticed there was more and more hair in my bathroom sink each day. My hair texture began to look frizzy and straw-like. One morning, the shock I experienced when I witnessed that a whole chunk of my long hair had fallen on to my pillowcase led me to the conclusion that it was high time for a shave. I wanted to be proactive and in control, so I opted to have my hair gone before I started to look like a rabid animal with alopecia.

Unlike some cancer patients, I did not have a head-shaving ceremony or party. I also want to point out that not all chemotherapy treatment will lead to hair loss. In my case, the platinum-based chemicals used would for sure lead to hair loss. I merely had my husband, daughter, and my long-time hairdresser, Maria, present. I looked in the mirror while Maria skillfully brushed my thinning hair, seeing chunks and chunks of loose but dead hair. At once, I knew this was the right thing to do. There were no tears from all present at the shaving. I studied my new shiny head and was impressed with my bald look.

Cancer patients could either look at their naked noggins and see the baldness as heroic or feel like hard-done-by victims. Instead of seeing an image of a sufferer, I saw a strong warrior, a fighter with a rebellious badass attitude. Being bald was liberating, and I was empowered to own my cancer. I knew Keith did not feel I lost my femininity; all he could see was his beautiful wife. Similarly, Gigi did not even notice the hair was gone because all she could see was her gallant mother with a slick new airbender look. We were all laughing and celebrating this new sensational look. The haircut reminded me of Sigourney Weaver in the movie *Alien*.

When I attempted to pay my hairdresser, she refused to accept it. That was when my tears started to stream down my cheeks, but I would wear my baldness with pride! I also learned that many hairdressers had a code not to charge a cancer client, and it touched me deeply. Similarly, I recalled when my brother, Richard, had to bury his thirteen-month-old baby on Christmas Eve. The funeral director did not collect a penny for his services. There are a lot of kind-hearted professionals who treat people in distress with great benevolence, and I have undying respect for their compassion.

On social media, there has been a debate about whether head-shaving fundraisers have become an "offensive" or "charity-porn" publicity. In the history of humankind, people have shaved their hair to demonstrate solidarity for a common cause. Does shaving one's hair support a loved one in the cancer journey? Will a friend or family member's shaved head alongside the cancer patient eliminate the bone-crushing pain, fatigue, or queasiness? Such a kind intention intended as a supporting gesture might inadvertently minimize the reality of cancer pain. Although Gigi asked whether she should also get a shave, I thanked her for her support but advised her not to join the club. The act of asking to join was the most considerate offer, and one has to contemplate how a cancer patient would feel having to be surrounded by baldness. For me, it would have traumatized me further if I had to carry the guilt of getting sick. Despite my advice, Gigi found a loophole and donned a pixie cut anyway.

Cancer is obviously more than just losing a person's hair. Hair was often a beautiful and significant part of my childhood. The memory of my mom yelling to get my long hair braided before school is a trigger of childhood memories. I was extremely resistant to getting my hair braided. To an extent, my long hair was my identity and a reminder of my childhood's endless irreverent behaviors. The memories of me as a young impish child, running around in the kitchen with a hairbrush in my hand, while my mother and godmother tried to apprehend me to tie my hair after a shower, came flooding back.

My godmother was a kind woman who was also my mother's closest friend. My siblings always referred to my godmother as "O' Yee," which means *dear auntie* in Fujian, a dialect used in the Fujian province in the south of China. Being able to be crowned as an "auntie" in a Chinese family is the pinnacle of honor. When O' Yee had both her legs amputated due to diabetes, as an adult, I could not bring myself to visit her while she was at the hospice. My family was puzzled why I was so cold-hearted by not visiting a dying woman who had dedicated her life to my family ever since I was born.

I am now able to explain the wall I created to protect myself emotionally. My godmother was a very poor woman who lived in a tiny hut along the riverbank of my childhood hometown. She played a major part in my youth, and she was the only nanny I ever had. I used to be fascinated by her little wooden hut, which stood on four posts on top of the muddy river known as Batu Pahat river. The little hut was a house for multiple families. I loved having sleepovers at her house, and my mother would often let me walk home with her when she was done with the chores at my family home. O' Yee's little hut had no electricity nor running water. To save money, O' Yee never turned on her oil lantern at night, but I enjoyed spending those dark nights at her house.

One night, I stayed over at O' Yee's home. I remembered that I could see through her wooden planks on the bedroom floor. I was able to see gleaming catfish flapping in the mud through the wooden planks of her room. Most excitingly, I was able to capture fireflies in a mason jar to keep the dark hut bright. Fireflies are common in tropical countries and are often abundant near the riverbanks. Whilst I grew up in a relatively well-off environment, being able to see how people endured poverty in contrast to my upbringing was an educational journey for me.

O' Yee's husband was either handicapped or complacent. He did not work and was always lying on the floor in his underpants smoking his "medicine" in a long pipe. I was wondering whether he had a drug addiction which caused him not to work. The rumor was that he was involved in a severe truck accident and never recovered. My poor O' Yee single-handedly brought up and educated her four children. As a young kid, I had much empathy and love for my O' Yee and vowed that I would take care of her when I became an adult.

The next morning, I was unable to find my flip-flops, which I wore to my godmother's hut. Flip-flops stealing was a common episode in the poor area. Taking off our shoes is a sign of respect, and I had to leave my flip-flops in the communal entranceway. The journey from my godmother's house to my family home was a good two miles of rocky unpaved roads. My O' Yee did not want to hurt my little snow-white feet, so she flipped me over her shoulder and carried me on her back.

It was a scorching Malaysian tropical day in the midday sun, and I was not small. My O' Yee was a strongly built farmer. She grew up in communist China and had no second thoughts about carrying a stocky toddler on her back with the noon sun beating down. As we strolled past a coffin-making carpenter, my O' Yee let me down gently so she might fit me with a pair of wooden clogs made of the wood hollowed out from the coffin-making process. I knew at that moment, this godmother of mine was the most altruistic person, whose love for me was stronger than the mighty river. Even though this event occurred some fifty-five years ago, I still could remember vividly the color of those wooden clogs – they were bright red with orange stripes.

When I found out O' Yee had lost both of her legs, she was in palliative care in a makeshift retirement home. I had since emigrated to America and had not seen my godmother for more than twenty years. The sorrow and conflict in my mind were that I could not face a godmother who used to carry me on her back without legs. I wanted to preserve the perfect memory I had growing up in her care. I never visited her once, and she passed, but I was told she passed away peacefully in the crowded and blistering retirement home. The image of her weakened ending would have traumatized me. I would have regretted visiting her because I wanted to have her living in my head as the tall Chinese farmer-nanny who was resilient and full of life. I never wished to alter that image of the woman who devoted her youth to caring for me. I would always remember her being so proud of her two gold-covered front teeth as she smiled, wearing her traditional Chinese flowery blouse and her matching colorful and yet baggy trousers.

The point of diverting this chapter to my godmother is that I understood how different caregivers reacted uniquely to cancer patients and their suffering. Although my husband and daughter openly praised my baldness and told me I had a beautiful egg-shaped head suitable for the front page of *Vogue*, I also understood the cocktail of emotions in my daughter, who was used to seeing my luscious long hair. She was probably very likely hurting inside seeing my hair being shaved. I also learned that as a cancerous mother, I would never use my child to be my emotional crutch.

When I first met with Dr. Cerise – my book-writing coach – about including a chapter on head-shaving for this book, she confessed to me that that she was present at her mother's head-shaving due to breast cancer some eighteen years ago. She admitted that if she could turn the clock back, she would have rather avoided seeing her mother's hair being shaved. I started to wonder whether my husband and daughter felt the same way but just never expressed their feelings.

I want to remind fellow cancer patients that in most cases, whoever is caring for us will face a hard time in dealing with this despicable disease. Your loved ones or friends might have experienced losses by cancer in the past. Seeing a bald head might remind them of the loss. Cancer did change me physically, intellectually, and emotionally. Cancer patients might feel empowered by shaving their hair, bragging about saving hair care products, feeling free, etc., but the truth was, if my loved ones were brave enough to be present during my head-shaving, they must love me immensely to witness it.

Hair loss via cancer was traumatic, and it was certainly an event I would rather not put my young daughter through. At the same time, to understand the patient's grief would be to avoid saying "Don't worry, your hair will grow back." After the initial shock of shaving my head, I did have to take a minute to embrace the new look, and sometimes no words can be better than saying some compliments. When I won the lottery of cancer, I said nothing to my daughter, and when I lost my hair, I said even less. The silence was peaceful, and it allowed me to cry from the inside.

Chapter Eight

The Naming of My Tumors

*"D*o I not destroy my enemies when I make them my friends?"
– Abraham Lincoln

Many of my friends were humored by the names I gave to my tumors and were also curious as to how those names arose. In my days living in the United Kingdom, there was a very popular comedian by the name of Rowan Atkinson, CBE, who did a comedic sketch called, "The Devil (Toby) welcomes you to Hell." I gave my tumor a human name so I might be seen to be in control and able to change the way I interacted with it. This act was the opposite of naming a beloved pet or a much-admired car. If I named my tumor, I was the boss.

When I was diagnosed, I was in immediate denial that my predicament was real. So, instead of acknowledging the reality I had yet to wrangle with, I denied the C-word in my vocabulary and chose to label this repulsive tumor as "Toby" just like the devil. A very dear work colleague of mine had inadvertently called it "Tory." Coincidentally, I needed another name for the second tumor that was discovered on the left side of my lymph node. This new tumor was ever so slightly softer and smaller in size; therefore, I adopted the much gentler name "Tory" for it, thus saving embarrassment for my work colleague and not needing to correct her. I hope when she reads this chapter, she will be quite amused, and I should perhaps tell her she needs a pair of reading glasses to go along with her retirement.

Many of my daughter's classmates from Columbia University were aware of my diagnosis, and quite a few of them had followed me on Instagram. They chose to refer to me as "DMJ," short for Doctor Mama Jo as a term of endearment. As the origin of my tumors' names was not explained, one of my adopted sons from Columbia had speculated that I acquired the name "Toby" from the popular TV sitcom *The Office*. There was an annoying and petulant character called "Toby" in *The Office*. On social media, my supporters started a hashtag – #TobyGoingDown – as a form of support and solidarity.

It is often said that the cancer world is the worst place to meet the best people. I have since found out that I am not the only person who named their tumors. A cancer warrior was more polite than me, and her tumor was called, the Little Blighter, just like an English term to refer to something impish and a nuisance. Another fellow cancer warrior named her tumors Chucky, with the formal name of Charles Lee Ray, the serial-killing doll that wreaked havoc in the *Child's Play* series of movies. How appropriate the name Chucky was, since he did torture this cancer patient for a long time. As I was writing this chapter, I found out my fellow cancer warrior had passed away. Sadly, Chucky did suck the life out of her, and she departed peacefully in her husband's arms.

Chapter Nine

Dying While Still Alive

"*K*eep going. Never die easy." - Unknown

In a cancer patient's life, pain is inevitable, but I believe suffering can be made optional. Above all, cancer does not come with a handbook. One must also understand that each patient reacts to treatment in a unique way and no two cancers are alike. Apart from the hair loss, I suffered virtually no side effects from my first chemotherapy. I remember bragging to myself that chemotherapy was a breeze and a cakewalk until the cumulative impacts of chemotherapy number two, three, four, etc. showed their ugliness.

On the day I completed my second chemotherapy, Keith and I decided to fly home to care for my daughter due to her recent knee surgery. The flight home was easy since my body was loaded with anti-inflammatory medicines. As the day went by, I was still boasting about how easy chemotherapy was, but in the middle of the night, I experienced some chest pains and heart palpitations. Our immediate instinct was to take me to our local hospital where my IVC filter was installed.

The initial assessment of my chest pains was a feeling that it was another episode of a blood clot given the history of my first thrombosis. Upon further chest scans, doctors confirmed that I had multiple tiny blood clots lingering on my IVC filter and some evidence of pulmonary embolism in my right lung. I spent the next three days connected to a twenty-four-seven Heparin – blood thinners – infusion. The experience was strenuous and draining. I began to realize how aggressive Toby was. Toby was being belligerent and antagonistic by creating more random blood clots that could kill. I also came to the realization that this chemical warfare with Toby was going to be an uphill struggle.

After numerous consultations from the various hospital doctors, there were some confusing recommendations, including the removal of the IVC filter. The hematology experts believed the IVC filter was causing the blood clots, but the cardiology experts insisted the filter prevented me from having a stroke or heart attack. Without a conclusion, I was discharged. No medical experts could provide or elaborate on the root cause of these haphazard blood clots, but the clique of doctors in my local hospitals did seem to be very proficient in pointing fingers at one another. The different teams of experts at my local hospital did not inspire confidence. Argument among the doctors in front of me was not a way to inspire a somewhat dazed cancer patient. That was when I realized that I needed to return to the one-stop shop at MD Anderson to further my treatment.

At that point, I was reminded of one of our friends who had lost his father to pancreatic cancer. When my friend found out I had a second episode of blood clots, he cautioned me that most people thought he lost his father to pancreatic cancer, but actually it was pulmonary embolism caused by blood clots. This message resonated with me, and I knew that in order to win this battle with Toby, I must keep my blood thin and not succumb to Toby and his sneaky below-the-belt attacks. This reinforced my position that I needed to be surrounded with a team of cancer experts who work together to fight this battle and orchestrate the best outcome for me.

The nurses at my local hospital were all very caring and well-trained during an extremely difficult and risky time to be a nurse but in the excitement of disconnecting my IV, the nurse had momentarily forgotten about my super-thin blood after seventy-two hours of blood-thinners. As she pulled my IV line out, blood gushed out and almost hit the ceiling. On the verge of panic, I could only laugh as it decorated the ever-so-boring white of the hospital room! There was frantic cleaning activity, which would always amuse me and bring a savage grin to my face. A day or two after being discharged from my local hospital, Keith and I flew back to Houston for an appointment for my third chemotherapy.

Looking back, our decision to seek cancer treatment at MD Anderson was clearly the right decision and, as it turns out, the most optimal plan. The inconvenience of living away from our own home might have been bothersome, but I soon learned that feeling homesick pales in significance to the opportunity to work with cancer experts.

Chapter Ten

The Singing Surgeon

"*L aughter and tears are both responses to frustration and exhaustion. I myself prefer to laugh, since there is less cleaning up to do afterward."- Kurt Vonnegut.*

When I returned to Houston with my multi-colored arms from the various IVs, the medical team recommended that I should have a chemotherapy port. As is known, the long-term use of veins for chemotherapy is not sustainable. My medical team agreed that I should have my chemo-port installed before scheduling my next infusion.

I was very lucky to be assigned to Dr. B, a man with a reputation for being a humorous surgeon who specialized in inserting chemotherapy ports. Dr. B came to visit me before the surgery and asked which side of the chest I would prefer for the port but then proceeded to inform me that the right side would work best for me. He then asked for my husband's cell phone number, and he picked up the landline in the patient room to place a personal call to Keith just to inform him all was well, and that the surgery was about to commence. That was just one of the extra mindful touches from Dr. B during a time of COVID-19 when, typically, hospital patients were deprived of a family escort.

In a heartbeat, I was wheeled to the surgery room. The mischievous part of me asked the transport technicians to race on the four-wheeled hospital bed. I often wondered just how many four-wheeled hospital beds had collided in such a huge hospital. I recall, while I was living in England, there was an annual Great Hospital Bed Race in Knaresborough. I am not sure this would work on the streets of Houston though.

In the surgical room, there were multiple technicians and nurses. However, most importantly, there was music. The surgery was an awake procedure. Before I was locally sedated, Dr. B asked me to name a few of my favorite songs. I voted for "Fly Me to the Moon" by Frank Sinatra.

While nurses and technicians readied the sterile space, an instrumental music came on. I could hear Dr. B's crisp and professional singing voice serenading me in this spa-like nightclub. Before I was able to applaud, the surgery was completed. Dr. B then switched gears to a new but upbeat Frank Sinatra song, "I Got You Under My Skin," as he stitched me up. I distinctly recall that I was invited to sing along during the surgery. If I had a piano or viola with me, we could have been an orchestra that day. I understand that most surgeons prefer music in the operating room not just to mask the noise of the surgical tools clinking sound, but it also helps to set the mood and encourage concentration. It has been said that surgeons make stitches much more neatly if they work in a relaxing atmosphere. Dr. B's live performances were definitely the sine qua non!

As Dr. B concluded the surgery, there was loud karaoke music of ABBA's "Thank You for the Music." I remember both nurses, surgeon, and patient rocking and singing in unison celebrating a successful procedure. I was glad that a doctor could invest so much in the mental health of his patients through his amazing voice. I truly did not feel like an unwell patient. That was one of the many ways that MD Anderson helped to make my cancer a bit less threatening.

Chapter Eleven

Happy Smile, Injured Body

"You got to look good to feel great." – Josephine Spence
    After my third round of chemotherapy, my hands began to shake like a drunken sailor that had been deprived of alcohol. In theory, I should have felt like a being devoid of joy, but I was very skillful in putting on a brave face. The disguise I wore was also my way of minimizing distress for my loved ones. My complexion was yellow and anemic, and I scared my sister one morning when I ran into her without any makeup. I regret scaring her the way I did. Friends who saw me during my treatment periods asked how I managed to look so good being a cancer patient, and here is my explanation.

I woke up every day and looked in the mirror before I could face any fellow humans. All I could see was a plain hard-boiled egg for a face and a fully bald monk-like head. Every single strand of hair, all over my body, was gone. My face had lost my once chubby chins; instead, it was covered with creased skin. My neck appeared to be as attractive as a turkey neck, complete with scars from my IVC filter and my port for infusions. The scars seemed to be permanent and got more prominent as more body weight was lost. The look might be suitable for Lord Voldemort, but it certainly did not qualify for the cover of *Women's Health* magazine.

I loved cosmetics and always was a big fan of dressing up to look great. I was resilient and very determined to put on full-face makeup regardless of what appointment I had that day. The last comment I wanted to hear was "You look sick!" .

When I got out of bed every morning, I would lock myself in the bathroom to work out a game plan on how to make myself look like a human. I had to admit when my hands were shaking, it was virtually impossible to hold my eyeliner straight, let alone apply my false eyelashes with a steady hand. Somehow, I was persistent and was able to get a good look for my plain face. With each attempt at eyeliner that went sideways, I responded with another try to get it right with my rickety right hand, and perseverance became my middle name. At one point, I even mastered the use of my left hand. That was when I invented an ambidextrous version of myself.

I told myself, *if you can't beat them, join them*, a pale face on top of a pale face was a great way to hide my sickness, and nobody needed to notice the painful melancholy I was trying to hide. My family members had all heard of many horrible aftermaths that chemotherapy could lead to, but I was not in a position to candidly show my loved ones what chemotherapy pains a cancer patient had to endure. Deep down in my heart, I knew happiness and health were the best makeup. When I became cured, my beauty would stem from my glowing happiness within.

The moral of this chapter is to quote one of Monty Python's songs, "Always Look on the Bright Side of Life." When life looks hopeless, that is when we all should laugh and dance. Cancer depression was never in my dictionary. How would cancer patients get encouraging and happy vibes if they surrounded themselves with negative and sad thoughts?

Snow White and the Seven Dwarfs said, "Whistle while you work," and I said, "Whistle while you are being infused or radiated." Whenever I entered the radiation room, I would ask for the music of ZZ Top to be played because loud but happy music drowned out the sounds of the machines. It also scared Toby because I am convinced Toby hated the beat of Frank Beard's drums. This little band from Texas was and are my cheerleaders day in, day out, and I feel the aura of joyfulness whenever I hear their songs.

Chapter Twelve

Mighty River of Love

"For the sick it is important to have the best." – Florence Nightingale

As I was being treated in Houston during the peak of the COVID-19 pandemic, the chance of my family members visiting from Asia was slim to none. Air travel was highly restricted due to COVID-19.

I grew up with eleven siblings. There was no doubt all my siblings had some fights and familial rivalry among us when we were young children, but I never wished to be an only child at any point in my life. When I found out about my diagnosis, there was an urgent need to share the news with all my siblings, but not with my elderly mother. I knew all my brothers and sisters would be most sympathetic and supportive. Given the distance and COVID-19 restrictions, we formed a group chat line on WhatsApp. There were days that I could not bear the cancer pains and my only outlet was a long chit-chat with my brothers and sisters. At the same time, all of us agreed not to inform my mother, who was approaching ninety-eight years at that time. My goal was to get well enough so I might deliver the news in person.

My second sister, whom we call S. Kuan, is six years my senior. I grew up under her wing since she always took care of me and was my algebra tutor when I could not accept what my middle school teacher had taught me that if you added X and Y, you could get the numeric value of ten. I was in a complete state of confusion and traumatized.

I came home arguing that mixing letters and numbers was not legitimate mathematics to S. Kuan, and she sat me down at our large home tutoring desk. She calmly explained to me that algebra was an art as well as a science.

With much persuasion and convincing, I agreed with S. Kuan that numeric and letter values did coexist in algebra. I recalled S. Kuan had to bribe me with a pair of her spectacles since she knew I had secretly worn them. I became excellent in algebra throughout my adult learning. I learned that questioning the logic of mathematics led me to the path of becoming an analytical thinker and a scientist.

My second sister was the one who made me believe algebra was the equivalent of music notes for mathematics. How could I ever not respect my second sister, who made me a strong mathematician? I would go around the school wearing those glasses not meant for me just to look smart. I have had extreme short-sightedness since before I reached puberty due to wearing a pair of avant-garde John Lennon glasses not prescribed for me. However, wearing glasses was my definition of happiness.

In the scorching summer of Houston, S. Kuan and her husband arrived at our rented apartment. We could not risk the COVID-19 exposure, so S. Kuan and brother-in-law had to hide in the second bedroom waiting for the home test kits to perform. I waited patiently in the living room for a century before I could hug my sister with floods of emotion. My longing for my mother's embrace during my very first chemotherapy was adequately addressed by hugging her. I longed for a physical connection with my family but had to wait for four months due to the chaos caused by the pandemic. I cried in my sister's arms for a long time when I saw her.

My relationship with S. Kuan was almost like a baby with a mother. S. Kuan is the most selfless and caring person, just like Florence Nightingale. She gave up her special time with her newly born granddaughter so that she could become my caregiver. To have Keith as the only person carrying the burden of nursing me would have been a smidge too far. I knew my occasional desire to end it all was a real concern for my husband, who was near his wit's end. S. Kuan and her husband became a vital support structure to Keith, who at this point of working long hours and caring for me, had become very exhausted.

The rented apartment we had near MD Anderson was on the forty-seventh floor with an easily accessible balcony. Whenever I looked out, I could sense my caregivers' anxiety. That was because I stated that it would have been easier to jump off the balcony than to have another round of chemotherapy. I was sure I was not myself when that statement was made. It was most likely due to the hallucinating medicines I was prescribed. If I recollected my state of mind during the peak of the treatment, I sometimes had wild mood swings. I would also scream when the pain was unbearable, probably waking up all my fellow neighbors.

The walls for these rented high-rise apartments were not thick or soundproofed. There were nights when I had to vomit repeatedly due to the strong cancer medication. It was hilarious and yet sad that some nights, I could hear my neighbors doing exactly the same. In a very discreet way, we probably all comforted each other knowingly through the thin walls. There would be my loud vomiting noise followed by the words "Oh, God!" and then miraculously my neighbor would throw up in sympathy followed by the words "Oh, shit!" or something similar. I also knew that my sister was a light sleeper; she must have heard all these "community vomiting" noises and shook her head in great sorrow because I noticed her eyes were always tired in the morning.

I wish I could turn back the clock and teach myself how to minimize the echoes of vomiting in the sparkly bathroom with tiled floors. Somehow, the quietness of the sparsely furnished bathrooms often served as the most acoustically-perfect room. Later on, I learned to blast music while I was vomiting. I knew this made me sound like a bulimic patient with an eating disorder. The matter of fact was the cancer drugs made this inevitable.

Other strange physiological side effects of chemotherapy and radiation were simultaneous constipation and diarrhea. My whole body was not intelligent or logical. One minute I was taking medicine for constipation, and the next minute I was taking Imodium to control diarrhea. It would appear that my brain and physical bodily functions were not connected. There was a constant uncoupling between what the brain said versus what the body would do. Perhaps chemotherapy created a form of cognitive dissonance in me. My bodily functions were sometimes like a newborn baby in diapers and occasionally living in a world of a dementia-ridden old person.

My sister was profoundly caring and competent. Even though she was not a trained nurse, she took care of my every need where she saw fit. Knowing my appetite was a bit of a hit-and-miss, my sister would shrewdly place food around the apartment with the hope that I would feel the urge to consume. Never once did my sister became obtuse or impatient with my peculiar needs. In retrospect, I was quite a difficult patient to care for because my emotions were profoundly confusing to those who cared for me. I was glad I had a sister identical to Mother Teresa, who loved me unconditionally.

I did pray my cancer never returned, but should it rebound, I would always want S. Kuan by my side because she understood what cancer did to my personality, cognitive abilities, and mindset. Her perpetual faith in God always lifted me when I was at the bottom of the barrel. Throughout the summer, S. Kuan was just as patient with me as when I was the middle school kid who refused to accept algebra!

Surrounding myself with people who propel positive energy was very important to me. Inevitably, I saw some sad and unpromising cases in the Houston Medical Center. For example, there were some water fountains in Houston Park, and I once saw a cancer patient. She appeared to be homeless because her worldly goods were in an H.E.B. grocery store cart, packed full of plastic bags to keep her warm at night. (H.E.B. was a grocery store near the medical center). She had no place to shower, and I saw her standing in the water fountain to get washed. To be going through cancer and be homeless must be the worst curse.

The US healthcare system has its detractors, but seeing this homeless person treated by MD Anderson gives hope that many things do work well. That was when I reminded myself that I was blessed to have financial security to help me cope with my illness. Most importantly, I had my family members, who shared my load.

When I was a frequent flyer at the infusion center, on several occasions, I saw another elderly cancer patient who would line up to receive her infusion, pushing her belongings in a grocery cart as she checked in for her chemotherapy. Unlike the other homeless cancer patient, this old lady appeared to be more well-equipped. Her worldly goods consisted of a woven blanket made of used plastic bags. Somehow, she must have taken her time to convert those used plastic bags into a blanket. She would always beg for hospital food, knowing that the infusion center often provided a ham or turkey sandwich with cheese between the extra thick Texan doorstop white slices of bread. I might have often rejected the free sandwiches at the infusion center, but I occasionally thought about those who lived under the Houston highway bridges with no family to share the burden and cried. I vowed to myself that if I ever ran into that homeless patient again, I would share with her my last bowl of rice.

People who have brothers and sisters often overlook how lucky they are. Sure, occasionally there are sibling rivalries, but I always knew there was always someone there for me when I returned home from school as a kid. All my siblings had an unspoken understanding of each other because we had been brought up the same way and received our parental attention equally.

I was the tenth child of my parents' herd of offspring, and there were some age gaps between myself and all three of my sisters. I grew up a tomboy under the influence of my elder brothers who were closer in age to me. My fifth brother, C. Kang, was always cooking up some adventures, which would get us in major trouble. He was the one who let me tag along with him when he went catching tiny mud crabs in the ditches. He also taught me how to catch golden spiders in little matchboxes to train them how to win a spider wrestling match with our neighbors' kids.

C. Kang was a quiet boy, but full of original ideas. He was always up to no good but seldom got caught red-handed. When we were young, I would follow him everywhere. On one occasion, he managed to lay his hands on a little sampan boat from our cousin, and he took me into the tropical jungle to observe monkeys in their natural habitat. I remembered being inches away from a whole gang of swinging monkeys in the thick jungle, and it was the most fun I had as a kid. There was only one minor detail we overlooked: we forgot to inform anyone where we were going.

When the police search party came looking for the two missing kids, we were in so much trouble with my parents and older brothers. My family has a traditional and hierarchical structure, so the elder kids got to spank the younger siblings. C. Kang and I never got spanked, but I remember there was no dinner that night after the search and rescue team brought us home with our tails between our legs.

One Chinese New Year, my father's office was closed for the holiday season. I followed C. Kang like a faithful lap dog. Whatever no good he was up to, I was sure to be there holding the smoking gun. It was very quiet in my father's warehouse of coffee beans. C. Kang decided we were going to assemble a bomb to simulate the firecrackers for Chinese New Year. We were adventurous but unaware of the hazard, and our bomb was a success. Unfortunately, C. Kang accidentally set the homemade bomb in my father's warehouse.

Boooombang!

When it went off, the white ceiling became jet black with a blaring cloud of powder like a mushroom of rising clouds. C. Kang and I looked at each other while our faces were covered in black powder as if we were children laboring in the coal mines. The bomb made our hair look similar to Einstein's iconic mane but covered in specks of dusts. Not wanting to be disciplined, C. Kang and I took each other's hands and ran as fast and far away from the crime scene.

When my father attempted to figure out what happened to the warehouse ceiling, we did not confess, and we were economical with the truth. C. Kang and I washed off the evidence from our hands and face as if nothing had happened. When C. Kang and I became adults, I did then confess to my father it was my doing and never dragged C.

Kang into the confession. That was what I called a sibling bond and a benign family secret!

I have a younger brother, C. Kian, who is two years my junior. C. Kian was a sickly child who always wore his yellow wool jacket, constantly sniffling and asthmatic. My mother would task the elder siblings to babysit my youngest brother, who was always covered in snot due to his endless allergies. I often questioned my parents' sanity for having this youngest son since they already had me as the perfect tenth kid. Among our siblings, we often thought my youngest brother was a major accident since he was often poorly and was born with eleven fingers and thumbs. Somehow, we all grew to accept and love him since he was a blessing to our family.

Whether my parents accidentally produced their eleventh child, no longer do I doubt he was sent from heaven to bless our family. I am forever grateful and sanctified to have a younger brother because he is so pure and loyal to our family. As time passes, C. Kian has become the closest son to my aging father and mother. He made a lot of personal career sacrifices so he could dedicate his time to take care of my parents when most of other siblings had moved far away from them. I do want to say, I am no longer the perfect tenth child, but my younger brother is entitled to be crowned the most devoted son. If we ever need a definition of the Confucian teachings of filial piety, we merely have to reference my brother. I am forever indebted to C. Kian for being a consistent caregiver for my parents.

For the last thirty-five years, my sixth brother and younger brother have lived right next door to my elderly mother and father. When my father was ill and near death after years of diabetes, my two brothers were the key caretakers day in and day out. Together with their wives and children, they formed an indestructible arrangement so that neither of my parents would go without food or care. Whilst all my siblings respect our traditional filial piety education and cultural values, none of us could surpass what these two brothers demonstrated.

In our family, it is traditional that elder siblings take care of the younger ones. My mother tasked the four sisters to take my youngest brother for new shoes because his feet were always growing faster than his body. My younger brother had been a mere toddler at the time. Armed with the exact cash needed from Mom, we four girls carried our baby brother to the only shoe shop we had in our little town. When we showed the new shoes to my mother, they were rejected because my mother was concerned, they would not last long; after all, our baby brother was having a growth spurt. All four sisters went back to the shop and begged for a larger size as a replacement, and reluctantly, the shop owner let us make the exchange but in a different color. He gave all four girls a good telling off, and we were scolded hard.

But again, the second pair was rejected by my authoritarian mother.

We four sisters were scared to return these second pair of shoes since we had been reprimanded by the owner. To get creative, we went home to break open our piggy banks and collected all the coins we possessed to go back to the shop for a third pair of shoes. After committing such an act to hide the truth, all of us then had the job of hiding the un-returned second pair. We collaborated and decided to hide them in my father's filing cabinet, and no one was to spill the beans ever.

Twenty years later, when my father moved out of his office, somehow the tiny shoes were uncovered from his filing cabinet. We all laughed and giggled at this reminder of our childhood solidarity. That was how tight our family was. We never sold anybody out or betrayed one another and clearly, such a close-knit relationship lives on and on.

My sixth brother, C. Tee, is two years my senior. Growing up together, we attended the same middle school in our hometown. Unlike me, C. Tee was not brilliant academically at school. However, C. Tee had my father's good looks and often walked into our school with swagger. His hair was unconventionally curly, unlike all his Chinese classmates. Very often my brother would go to school wearing his white sneakers with the back heels folded because he was too lazy to bend down to straighten them. With his hair and with his unique way of wearing sneakers, I was somewhat embarrassed when schoolmates pointed out that he was my sibling.

My father was a big fan of Mercedes-Benz. As soon as C. Tee was old enough to drive, my father let him use one of his spare Mercedes to drive us to high school. Short of wearing a bag over my head, I would always hunch down in the back seat so no one could see me arriving at school together. My old high school was built on a small hill. C. Tee would drive all the way up the hill during the morning assemblies, while thousands of students and teachers were in the morning assembly along the hill. C. Tee craved attention and would enjoy all eyes on us, dragging this old Mercedes painted in James Bond gold with a noisy gearbox that squawked like a rusty violin as he dragged his sorry backside to attend the morning assembly.

C. Tee and I fought a lot as kids and teenagers. I used to swear he was not my real brother and spread a rumor that my mother must have salvaged him from a dumpster as an abandoned newborn on her way to the wet market. Even though my dear brother was two years my senior, he could never tell which flip-flop was for his left or right foot, and I would always dig him out of his predicament to save him from embarrassment. C. Tee never liked to eat green vegetables and often got punished by my second brother for being rebellious. And so it goes, because of all these sibling fights, we became the closest brother and sister. He is someone I would trust with my firstborn, and I always have that extra ounce of love for him.

My eldest sister, Y. Kuan, is eight years my senior, so I did not have the joy of hanging around her when I was growing up. I do remember that Y. Kuan loved dancing and was very popular with her large audience of admirers.

My third sister, H. Kuan, is five years my senior, and she tried hard to convert me from a tomboy to a young lady. I remember H. Kuan used to put a hardcover book, the *Oxford English Dictionary*, on my head and attempt to educate me how to walk like a lady. H. Kuan is also very good with art and painting. I remember her personal cupboard at home was always packed full of beautiful supplies. When she was at school, my younger brother and I would secretly peek inside, but we never stole any as far as I can recall. At least, that's all I will admit here.

H. Kuan was very quiet and obedient. She is the one and only child who would stay close to my mother in the kitchen. I suppose that is why she is better than the rest of us at home economics and cooking. I recall that H. Kuan was asthmatic and suffered from severe nose bleeds. Since she was permanently on medication, and she sometimes became disgruntled with taking her prescriptions, I would offer to take her medicines in return for a colorful eraser from her school supplies.

When H. Kuan became a gorgeous teenager, there were a lot of interested young boys camping out at our house. H. Kuan would reward me with something like a pencil or a paintbrush, and I would be tasked with chasing those boys away before my father could scold H. Kuan for attracting so many admirers. Being an innocent young kid, my message to those pesky boys were, "My sister told me to tell you she is not home."

Our daily sibling call during my treatment days served as a constant reminder of some of the wayward things we did as kids. Chatting about our memories somehow diverted my attention from the torture of cancer. I treasured every group call we had, as if the calls were my lifeline. The idle and carefree chats brought back those warm and loving feelings among my siblings, and somehow, fifty-eight years later, such a close bond felt even closer than ever, which I shall describe as the mighty river of love.

Chapter Thirteen

Living Life in Color

"*That which does not kill us makes us stronger.*" – *Friedrich Nietzsche*

In general, chemotherapy and radiation are the two classic cancer treatments. While Toby tried to kill me, I was sure the chemotherapy was endeavoring to finish the job. It is sad but true that cancer patients often attribute all symptoms to the cancer medication. Many have said that the cancer treatment is often worse than the disease itself. I continued to lose weight. Every time I saw food, I would rather have my tongue flattened wafer-thin by a meat tenderizer than eat anything. My three bodyguards, also known as the Three Musketeers – Keith, my sister, and my brother-in-law – were my constant cheerleaders. My appetite was non-existent, and no food nor drinks were of any interest to me. In an inexplicable way, I would have the mental desire to ingest a whole cow for lunch, but when the food arrived, the appetite simply vanished. Whenever there was any sign of my awakening appetite, the Three Musketeers swiftly bundled me to the nearest French restaurant, which I used to love before the chemotherapy affected everything.

I would boast to my bodyguards that I planned to swallow a twelve-ounce steak without vomiting. The cheers from these three highly excitable individuals would lead to several massive nutritious dishes being ordered. I was a trickster; I desired the food but could not physically ingest the food, just like the spirit was willing, but the tongue was not. Food tasted like winter rats stewed in cat vomit and dowsed in anthrax. Nightmares from my convent school reappeared. I thought all restaurant foods were cooked by the headmistress of the boarding school, Sister Consuelo – no flavor and disgusting. Meal after meal, there was lots of leftovers from restaurants. My weight went south, but my three bodyguards had jointly acquired a total of ninety pounds on my behalf.

Losing my basic bodily functions was the most embarrassing outcome of the treatment. My very first accident occurred while Keith and I were traveling in our rental car after picking up my sack full of medicines. For an adult woman to be unable to distinguish between farting and defecating as the most preposterous experience. It was humiliating and crushing for my self-esteem. At a certain point in time, it was virtually impossible to make a round trip to Costco without being close to the nearest bathrooms. I could also affirm that all those extra-secure diapers could not prevent me from soiling myself. At those moments, my self-esteem was at an all-time low. I can write about it now, but during those dark instances, I wanted to end it all. It was both exasperating and despairing.

During the radiation phase of the treatment, apart from the persistent and relentless fatigue, vomiting was also very frequent. One sunny day in Houston, I told Keith that I was nauseous. Keith suggested that we go for a drive to get some fresh air. So, Keith, S. Kuan, my brother-in-law, and I bundled into our rental car. As Keith was driving down the circular path from the parking lot, I saw a sewer drain, and I yelled to stop the car. As Keith stopped the car, I jumped out and proceeded to projectile vomit into the drain. I became so ashamed of myself for the complete loss of physical control of my body. Well, I did not make it to a toilet, but the sewer drain in the parking lot would do.

There were other side effects, such as a constantly runny nose. From the moment I got out of bed, my nostril drips would start, which gave others the impression I had a cold or COVID-19. Very often, the inside of my mouth would break out with sores. The sores were severe and located randomly from the roof of the mouth to the gums, causing my teeth to weaken and making chewing impossible. Most of those days, all I could eat was soup or ready-made protein shakes, or ice cream. I had to use a prescribed mouthwash commonly known as "magic mouth wash" to ease the rotten skin. Throughout all of this, Toby would cause unexplained ringing in my ears, and I would often lean to my right in a very unstable manner.

Ice cream and lollipops became my favorite mouth-sore cure. I never really drank alcohol but when the pain was too unbearable, Keith would slip a few alcoholic freeze pops for me as breakfast. Looking back, I did live a very unusual twenty months during that period. As the need to numb my mouth sores rose, our grocery list often included a large quantity of mango sorbet and coconut water. During our stay in Houston, we discovered quite a few ice cream parlors which we frequented. Indeed, to celebrate my very first radiation, we all went for a meal of ice cream. There were swings in that shop for little kids, and we all felt like life was much more tolerable when there was ice cream or sorbet. Although we did not get to sit in the swings made for children, in our hearts, we became young again.

Chapter Fourteen

The Killing of Toby

"*Seek revenge, and you should dig two graves.*" – *Unknown*

Our rented apartment was right next to the cancer emergency room. It was convenient and sidesplittingly funny that I could walk to the emergency room faster than getting our car out of the parking lot. After we got the blood clots under control using a daily injection of two doses of extra-potent blood thinners, I became very prone to bruises and bleeding. While it was very challenging to self-inject a four-inch needle twice a day, I was beginning to coexist with the needle marks on my stomach since it reduced the risk of pulmonary embolism. I could also affirm that having zero fat in the stomach made the injection process more agonizing. The medicine would slowly burn the skin with an excruciating and thorny sensation.

After my fourth chemotherapy with targeted monoclonal antibodies (Avastin) as part of the infusion cocktail, the medical attack plan started to take charge of Toby. The tumor started to bleed dispiritedly. The medicines aggravated Toby by deactivating the blood vessels that supplied nutrients to the cancerous cells. The assumption was that Toby was starving and in necrosis while bleeding itself out. The blood loss was demanding and fatiguing, and my white blood cells and platelets became too low. I was admitted to the cancer emergency room yet again for blood transfusions.

I had never had a transfusion, but I could say that allowing someone else's blood to go into my body was otherworldly. Those who donated to the blood banks to save my life have my undying respect. Coincidentally, a good friend of mine, Liz, was a frequent blood donor, and she has the same blood type as me. Liz and I would joke that I might have received one of the bags of her blood. Liz is another selfless and joyous friend to have around. Whenever I was in the ER, she would be there to support me. Little things she would do were sneaking an iPhone charger to the ER when I was rushed to the hospital without one. Liz would send over homemade zucchini bread or home-harvested organic honey to help build me up. These little gestures might have been perceived as trivial or of no significance by my friend, but they meant a great deal to me. Liz's true greatness was the ability to do seemingly small gestures that made a big difference.

During the heavy bleeding weeks, I was in bed most of the time to minimize further loss of blood. Thanks to Houston's beautiful skyline views, I was able to get some inspiration to soldier on staring at the miraculous sunrise and sunset from my bed. Those were my darkest hours, and at some point in time, I became somewhat religious and was constantly in conversation with my maker. As the cumulative side effects of chemotherapy peaked, my body was in persistent pain, where no words can describe the anxiety, I had. Unfortunately, I was not able to tolerate any of the painkillers since I reacted to them with instant vomiting.

During one of my numerous ER stopovers, my body was in so much pain that the ER doctor begged me to try the next level painkiller stronger than morphine. I explained to the ER doctor that painkillers, without exception, caused me to vomit. With the genuine desire to eliminate my agony, the ER doctor ordered the Fentanyl to be mainlined into my veins. My immediate reaction was to expel bodily fluid like a scene from *The Exorcist* within seconds of the drug arriving in my body. When my vomit flew straight onto the ER doctor's white coats and his glasses, I saw the last bastion of my decorum disappear. The embarrassment led me to apologize to the doctor by offering to pay for his dry-cleaning bill. I prayed secretly that thou shall not meet this doctor again in my next stopover at the ER.

At the latter stages of treatment, I was also unable to move my right arm due to muscle pains. The lack of use of my right arm inevitably led to a frozen right shoulder, which in turn prevented me from having dexterity on my right hand. During this phase of the treatment, the pain was intense, but I was comforted by the knowledge that Toby was suffering and dying. It gave me a great sense of satisfaction knowing he was meeting his demise. However, the medical team remained cautious until we knew Toby was truly obliterated.

Chapter Fifteen

Shifting My Treatment to Fifth Gear

"*Fall seven times, stand up eight.*" – *Japanese proverb*

After completing my neo-adjuvant chemotherapy, the scan did not show substantial shrinkage in the large tumor, Toby. We had another small tumor, Tory, traveling in the lymph node on my left hip. It started to look like platinum-based chemicals were about as useful as a cat flap in an elephant house. Since I had christened the large tumor as Toby, I decided to label the second tumor as Tory. After an agreement with my medical team, with a somewhat deflated outlook, Keith and I decided to take a mini-break and flew back home to get some fresh air while the cancer board re-strategized the plan of attack.

All quiet on the western front –not knowing the gameplan was going to be perturbing, and I was living with a sense of foreboding about what surprises Toby was going to throw at me next. During this halfway-house week, Keith and I returned home to regroup. Within one day of getting home, I received a personal phone call from my lead oncologist at MD Anderson. The doctor was almost apologetic and was probing whether I would be able to return to Houston for a new treatment strategy.

When my case was presented at the MD Anderson cancer board, one of the radiation oncologists, Dr. Klopp, raised her hand and questioned why we wouldn't treat my case like a colon-rectal cancer patient even though the source of cancer was endometrial. Since Toby was firmly attached to my colon and rectum - short of piercing into the organ walls – Toby was very much located in my colon and distorting my rectum. The radiation technology used for colon cancer could also work to shrink Toby.

I was on my grocery shopping trip when I received the call. There was no food at home in the pantry since Keith and I had been living in Houston. Grocery shopping was about my only relaxation. The call from MD Anderson led to excitement that was beyond description, and I abandoned my shopping trip immediately and headed home to arrange the first flight back to Houston. Without any hesitation, my sister, brother-in-law, and husband escorted me back to our rented apartment at Houston Medical Center.

Moving back to Houston with my three bodyguards was similar to the final scene in a war film. Whether the second plan of attack was granted with much faith of success was never discussed. My soldiers and I merely marched forward silently back to the front for the next battle, and I prayed and submitted my destiny faithfully to the one high above me.

Meeting Dr. Klopp was another life-changing event. Dr. Klopp is a down-to-earth radiation expert. The way she explained her plan was very clear and no-nonsense: we were going to attack the tumors using two types of machines. Tory was to be attacked using a CT radiation machine via an external beam, and Toby would also get a state-of-the-art MRL radiation machine based on the MRI scanning technology, also referred to as a linear accelerator in the physicist's world. Toby was an uncooperative tumor attached and adjacent to multiple vital organs, so the radiation had to be ultra-precise and mathematically accurate to minimize impairment to my functioning organs. In addition to the radiation, I would also receive weekly chemotherapy using Cisplatin as an agent. Some side effects from radiation would include diarrhea, bladder irritation, skin irritation, and possibly sexual dysfunction.

I wanted to begin this plan of attack as soon as possible. However, there was a mandatory pre-radiation planning week where they needed to pinpoint exactly where the radiation was to be administered. In my case, the radiation therapy team did a simulation where I received three tiny permanent tattoos as markers in my pelvic area. Like all radiation patients, a special body mold, known as Vac-Lock, was to be cast to fit my body so that I would be kept static during the radiation. The tiny tattoos on my pelvic area are almost invisible to the naked eye. I have to admit, I never really wanted a tattoo, and there I was getting three.

Looking back at the funny side of radiation preparation, while I was going through chemotherapy, my right shoulder and arm became "frozen," and I was not able to raise my right arm above my chin for the casting of the body mold. So, the best we could do was a shape which had my left arm high above my head and the right arm gently raised above my chin, looking very similar to the crime scene white chalk mark surrounding the outline of a dead victim. I thought to myself, my body mold could never be misidentified since it depicted my poor frozen right shoulder. I was glad to find out most body molds are recycled once the radiation courses are complete since there is only a finite number of radiation sessions a human body can endure.

In total, I had sixty-six — twice a day for thirty-three days — radiation sessions. For Tory, we attacked her with a short spell of laser lookalike beams using a CT machine and the tattoos on my skin to aim correctly. In most cases, I was able to request for the lights to be dimmed so that I could enjoy watching the green rays like a light show in the dark. To cover up the radiation machine noise, I was able to ask the radiation team to play ZZ Top's music.

For Toby, we bombarded him with an MRI intelligent radiation machine on a real-time basis. As tumors can shift as they grow or shrink, or when the living patient is breathing during radiation, the MRI linear accelerator measures and predicts the location needed to fire the radiation to minimize damage to other vital organs. I was calm and rested during the procedures. The MRI linear accelerator table was huge but friendly, covered in soft materials for comfort. The treatment room was very large, but most of the space was consumed by the state-of-the-art machine. The room plus the machine reminded me of the opening scene of *Superman*, and I was waiting for the Kryptonite and Marlon Brando to appear. It felt like I was in a fictional comic book.

As it turns out, even though I was alone in the MRI tube during the treatment, in reality, the radiation technicians were present in the adjacent monitoring room with the ability to communicate with me should I become distressed. Mo, my lead technician, always handed me my Kryptonite – the panic button – before he left me on the table. Mo and his team knew how to make me laugh. We always had our daily tease at each other before we got down to serious business. I was very dignified and self-assured before, during, and after my treatment until we arrived at my final radiation session.

It was the week before Thanksgiving, and Keith and I had hoped that we could return home. When I was in Dr. Klopp's office for a review and checkpoint, to my surprise, she indicated that she would like to run three more rounds of MRL radiation so that she could be certain that Toby was eradicated. Without a second thought, I agreed with her plan. We had to relocate our Thanksgiving to Houston. We flew Gigi out and celebrated in a hotel near the medical center.

I have to admit, on my very last radiation session, I was somewhat overwhelmed by the emotions of it all. The heavy and loud music of ZZ Top was not keeping me tranquil on that occasion. To Mo's surprise, I asked the music to be replaced with Tchaikovsky's "Swan Lake." Knowing that was my very last dose of radiation, I let myself feel the sadness, the distress, the excitement, the delight, and the ecstasy. Lying in the radiation tunnel, I had to reason with myself to get through the whole course, and I had.

I slept like an old cat for thirty-three days of radiation. The fatigue radiation delivered to my body was immense. I only woke up for food or vomiting, and those thirty-three days were a haze. Although radiation was somewhat easier to tolerate than chemotherapy in the short term, the effects lingered for at least twelve months or more. That experience made me re-watch the documentary on the Chernobyl disaster, and I have a small amount of understanding and an enormous amount of sympathy for what those victims went through during and after the disaster.

The hardest times often lead to the paramount moments in my life. As Marie Curie stated, "Nothing in life is to be feared; it is merely to be understood." As I was in the long tunnel for my very last radiation session, I closed my eyes and imagined Marie Curie in the MRI rays of hope. She represented how to live life with perseverance and confidence. Instead of my usual ZZ Top music request, I mentally held her hand listening to Tchaikovsky's "Swan Lake" as if she was guiding me through the last dose of radiation in person. I savored every second of the radiation knowing that my body would not be entitled to any more radiation for the rest of my life.

It might have been the excitement or anxiety that overtook me, but after my favorite radiation technician, Mo, painstakingly measured the exact spots to fire my very last MRI radiation, I developed an urgency to scratch my left leg, which I never did during my previous thirty-two days of radiation. I pressed the panic button, and Mo came rushing into the radiation room.

I informed Mo that I needed to scratch my left leg, and Mo held my hand and said, "You have done so well thus far, and we've never had to pause the radiation. Do you need to scratch? If so, I will have to restart the process because for you to move would invalidate the measurement we just did."

Deep down, Mo knew I had a psychological block in me that caused me to panic on my last ride. I requested Mo to turn up the music so I might contain my panic, and that was what assisted me to overcome my anxiety. We resumed and completed my last radiation.

I was proud of myself for being able to celebrate my emotions on my last day of radiation. If I had traveled this journey without honoring my emotions, I suspect I might have ended up dead inside. However, I was so glad that I let my final radiation be memorable. It felt that I had transformed all the darkness of cancer into light, and I was able to shed some tears, finally.

My type of cancer has a high probability of recurrence, so my lead oncologist decided that I would have fifteen more maintenance infusions just to be safe. After my last radiation, I was able to have a three-week break. Once we started the maintenance with targeted therapy, we were back living in Chicago, and I was flying to Houston every three weeks. Somehow, the frequent flights to Houston became a part of my routine, and I began to realize how lucky I was to progress into the maintenance phase of the treatment. Simultaneously, I concluded that I would let go of my previous career since I had been blessed enough to survive my deepest wounds. My resilience entailed accepting my new reality and my new identity. Somebody once said, "The old oak tree fought against the wind and broke, while the willow bent along with the wind and survived." Just like a willow branch or a canny sailor, I accepted I could not change the direction of the wind, but I could adjust my sails accordingly.

During the thirty-three days of radiation, my second sister, S. Kuan, accompanied me to the radiation center religiously. Just like when we were young, S. Kuan would walk me to school. We both enjoyed our daily walk from our rented apartment to the clinic at MD Anderson. We decided we needed to have some comfortable walking shoes, and to demonstrate our solidarity, we bought two pairs of identical hiking shoes. Monday to Friday, without fail, my sister would ensure I was suitably nourished before my radiation because she knew I would be so fatigued after the radiation, and she worried that I might inadvertently skip lunch and dinner because I was always fast asleep post-radiation. It was no exaggeration that I would enter the radiation with tons of enthusiasm and energy like a lioness but exited as a sleeping mouse. I have to admit, I once fell to sleep in the elevator between the ground floor to our forty-seventh floor abode.

On the weekends, Keith, S. Kuan, and my brother-in-law would try their very best to get me to do some walking because long period of sleep would increase my chance of blood clots. There were many excellent parks surrounding the MD Anderson buildings. We were also right next to the famous Rice University, where the campus was the most ideal for walking.

My brother-in-law loves tai chi, an ancient Chinese mind-body practice which appears to look like a slow-moving martial art. The journey to Rice University would entail a short stroll as a foursome packed full of jokes and laughter. We would often stop at the local help-yourself neighborhood libraries to exchange some old books. These libraries are homemade, see-through but weather-proof boxes stationed in most of the corners of the residential houses. It is an honesty-based system where a reader would donate a book before taking out another. Once the books are read, the readers would return the books to the same station. When we get to the beautiful campus of Rice University, my brother-in-law would do his tai chi exercises, and my sister and I would read while Keith went off to do his jogging. Since my brother-in-law looked like an expert in tai chi – and in reality, he is an expert – on a few occasions, the local Houston folks would come and video his exercises or solicit his number for a tai chi lesson.

I often look back at those eight months in Houston with my three bodyguards and smile. By some coincidence, my illness afforded me the opportunity to get even closer to my sister and her husband. They normally live in Hong Kong, and when they discovered the gigantic warehouses of Costco, the Houston way, they were like excited little children. We often treated our weekly visit to Costco like an excursion. Little things that did not make an impression on me prior to my illness had developed into significant life experiences stocked full of joy. Even a simple grocery trip became exciting for me because I was alive and was able to walk unaided. Somehow, I found liking what I do is the secret of happiness, even something as basic and simple as a grocery shopping excursion.

Chapter Sixteen

My First Wish

"You can never be overdressed or overeducated." – Oscar Wilde

The day when the doctors confirmed that I had advanced cancer, my immediate reaction was, "Whoa! Wait a minute. I have yet to attend my daughter's graduation." It was amazing how my brain instantly shifted into survivor mode and rushed into a frantic rundown of my bucket list. I asked my genie in a bottle to grant my first wish to be present at my daughter's graduation. When Gigi was born, she brought a whole new meaning to my life. Gigi is my only child, and the Holy Grail for me, as a mother, was to watch her walk across the stage and present her with a bouquet when she completed her undergraduate degree at Columbia University in New York.

Gigi is a very smart kid. At the age of three, after reading Beatrix Potter's *The Tale of Benjamin Bunny*, she acquired some big words of the English language. Every afternoon, after drinking her milk, she would often use the adult word *soporific* instead of *tired* when she wanted her afternoon nap. It was hilarious to see a young child sucking milk from a sippy cup and yet uttering a big English word.

When Gigi was six, we lost Keith's mother. While the ambulance was transporting Grandmother to the hospital, Gigi turned to me and asked, "Mommy, how many ancestors do we have now?"

I was often stunned and amused by such a little person with the ability to express herself so precisely and maturely. When she used to sit on her grandmother's lap to learn how to knit with her reading glasses due to her hyperopic eyesight, she reminded me of an old person inside a young child's body.

Not really being the stereotypical tiger mom, I lived for the moment she graduated from an Ivy League. Keith and I worked hard to be able to afford Gigi the once-in-a-lifetime opportunity of a Columbia education and I was not about to skip her graduation due to some annoying thing called cancer.

Dr. Westin at MD Anderson and I discussed long and hard how to schedule my treatment so I might attend Gigi's graduation. The years of the COVID-19 pandemic and lockdown had bottled up every graduate's anxiety. The commencement day finally arrived, and I was not going to let Toby inconvenience my plan in life. Keith and I flew to New York, and I was able to wear my skin-tight dress without needing two ostomy bags.

I have to admit, the commencement was very impressive, with a total of fifteen thousand attendees covering every single inch of the famous Low Beach outside the campus library. I felt some dampness on my cheeks, but not because of the spring showers in New York. I knew there and then, someone had heard my prayers and granted me this experience of being alive and sitting at Low Beach taking selfies with my newly minted Columbia graduate.

My daughter is a tenacious person and full of drive. When she was a mere three-foot preschooler, she was a child with few words and appeared to be constantly living in her own magical world. Gigi had inherited my strong will to survive or win, she has done some amazing things that confirmed she has my DNA.

There was a yearly rumble sale at her school called Mrs. Fitz's Rumble Sale, and Gigi saw a large doll that was two feet above her head. The school would give the students some vouchers to attend the market as a preview so little kids could have their first pick before opening the sale to the public. Even though Gigi was small in stature, she felt that large doll should go home with her. At that point, I was a full-time working mom, so Gigi would have to take the school bus, which transported her from her morning kindergarten to the afternoon school.

The image of her getting off the yellow school bus, lugging the doll double her size and walking up our steep linden tree-lined driveway was something I could never unsee nor erase from my memory. Although I was proud of my daughter the day she latched on for breast-feeding, the day when the large doll came home, I grew to ten feet tall, bursting with pride for my little girl. I was convinced she would go on and achieve great heights in life. I will always be Gigi's biggest fan and the loudest cheerleader. I have acquired my ninety-eight-year-old mother's strong survivor instincts, and I have an inkling such instincts have inadvertently passed on to my daughter.

Instead of engulfing herself in the sadness of my illness, Gigi became very solution-focused and supportive. My daughter knew how I enjoyed comedies, and seeing me laughing to classic sketches, she came up with a great way to cheer me up on a daily basis: Malaysian comedian known as Uncle Roger. She was sure that his comedic sketches would cheer me up. Every morning when I woke up, I looked forward to Gigi's instant message with side-splitting comedic sketches on my phone. Uncle Roger's trademark expressions of "Haiyaa" and "Fuiyooh" became my vocabulary whenever cancer hit me hard.

Gigi was finishing up her senior year of college in New York during the peak of my treatment in Houston. Each start of the school year, Keith and I would fly with Gigi to move her in for her first semester of the new college year, but that year I was too sick for the restart after the lockdown during the COVID-19 pandemic. Somehow, the long distance did not pull us apart. I felt Gigi's love and care each day she sent me hilarious jokes and mindless cat videos. Sometimes, it felt better to spare all the tiresome details of my suffering from my daughter because I never would want her to be burdened with my predicament.

As busy as it was for a senior at college, somehow, Gigi managed to give me a surprise visit on my birthday in Houston. Her desire to be with me was undoubtedly strong, and I swore to myself that there was a zero or next to no chance that I would miss her graduation ceremony – my upmost wish from my genie.

Many surprises hit me during two years of treatment. While Keith and I were looking the other way and busy with my cancer battle, Gigi became a grown woman. She received my diagnosis the week of her junior year final examination, but she took the news like a fearless soldier and battled on with her academic tests. As a full-time working mother, I did not teach her how to grow plants in the garden, iron a shirt, or cook rice, but Gigi taught me how to confront adversity with dignity. When I look back at her four years of college, Gigi had her left hip surgery in her first year, followed by her second surgery on her right hip, and another knee surgery in her third year. How Gigi survived the streets of New York clonking around with her orthopedic crutches during her college years remains a mystery to me. That is why I was the proudest mother on the day Gigi donned her pale blue Columbia cap and gown.

Chapter Seventeen

Sharing My Prognosis with My Mother

"Confession heals. The unhappiness is in not making the confession." – Unknown

I started writing a book about my beloved mother whom I adore. Somehow, my sickness got in the way of wrapping up my book about this marvelous and heroic mother of mine. My mother was born in 1920s China. My grandfather had a herd of daughters he could not afford to feed, and my mother was one of four girls. She is a four-foot-eleven-inch person. My mother was almost subjected to the torture of having her feet bound, a Chinese tradition, which would have made her waddle like a dainty and demure lady. Bound feet were perceived as a good breed for childbearing in those days, and it was unlikely that a girl would be able to run away from her future husband if her feet were equal to a three-inch pad. Her mother and father equated daughters to a financial burden since girls were believed to be too weak to help on the farm.

Moreover, it was believed only boys could perpetuate the family name. As a young toddler, her mother started to bind her feet by breaking her soft bones using cloth bandages. My mother fought against the torture, and my grandmother gave up. Although the foot binding attempt was a failure, it did leave my mother's feet very tiny, and she wears size two shoes.

My maternal grandfather had a close friend who was a sailor with no biological children. This close friend lived quite far away from my maternal grandfather, but when his ship docked at my mother's hometown, the two friends would reunite for some noodles and rice wine.

My grandfather's close friend was saddened that he could not have a child of his own, but he had an adopted son. When the adopted son was just about to enter school, his parents began to seek a child bride for him. Child brides were a common concept in those days in China. The beliefs were that in-home grooming and bringing up a child bride was better than allowing a stranger into the family. My grandfather's close friend was a kind man who loved his adopted children like his own kids. Unfortunately, the adopted daughter committed suicide by drowning herself in a pond near their home. As she was washing clothes, it was said that she was summoned by the devils who lived at the bottom of the pond, but the truth was that she was teased endlessly for being a child bride because it was synonymous with marrying one's brother. She ended her own life, and her departure devastated the old couple who adopted her.

Over some rice wine, the two friends decided to help each other. My grandfather needed to give up one of his daughters, and his friend needed a new daughter to cheer up his suicidal wife who had just lost her adopted daughter in such a tragic way. A mutually agreeable economic arrangement seemed reasonable to these two friends. So, my grandfather invited his friend to sit in his courtyard to observe his four daughters so that he could pick a girl to adopt.

The original plan was not to parade all daughters in front of the sailor friend; it was to give away my mother's eldest sister who had come to an age that was suitable for marriage and house chores. As the two friends were chatting in their courtyard observing my mother's eldest sister's superior ability to wash clothes and grind rice in a large mill made of stones, the deal was close to being done, but fate sent my mother – a younger child – to run across the courtyard while chasing her pet cat. My grandfather's friend asked whether my mother was available for adoption.

My grandfather took my mother to a local Chinese opera with his friend. With all the excitement and among a vast audience, my grandfather asked to be excused for a few minutes and requested my mother to stay with his friend. However, my grandfather never returned. My mother cried, screamed, and kicked, but her father never heard nor returned to collect her.

As a young girl of six, the fear of being abandoned must have had a major emotional impact. My mother's newly adopted father carried my mother to his ship, and they sailed back to my mother's newly adopted home. No conversation was had for weeks between my mother and her new parents because they did not speak the same dialect. The only way my mother could express herself was through tears.

My mother often told me how they showered her with love, but it could not compensate for a frightened six-year-old who feared the unknown. My mother thought if she could use a spoon and start to dig a hole in the ground, perhaps, when the tunnel was long and deep, she would be able to reconnect with her biological parents. The tunnel was never long or deep enough but my mother's loss of trust would linger for the rest of her life.

Since there was such a perceived shame for a child bride, my mother's adoptive mother did not desire for my mother to wed her adopted son. When my mother became a fifteen-year-old young lady, it was time to arrange for a suitor. My father was a young nineteen-year-old, fine-looking man newly returned from Singapore having escaped the Red Communists. Loke is my father's family surname. My father was not just attractive in person, but he was also nicknamed "Handsome Loke" because of his stunning good looks. My mother told me, there was a saying in their village that whenever Handsome Loke returned to the village, there would be multiple broken-hearted women due to my father's flamboyant presence and swagger of confidence with girls.

My adopted grandparents unearthed that my father's family was opulent given that his family was the sole producer of sea salt in the region of Fujian, China. The negotiated dowry was affordable and was very swiftly arranged. The innocent fifteen-year-old girl was outfitted in red as soon as the deal was struck. My mom was carried away to the next village in a six-man sedan chair accompanied by her dowry, consisting of a pig, goat, and some pork lard, to be married to my father.

In those days, marriages were mere economic arrangements between two families – falling in love was not essential. My parents had never met in person, let alone dated before the wedding. Falling in love before marriage was also taboo. The very first time they laid eyes on each other was the moment my father took off my mother's red silk veil on their wedding night.

On my mother's wedding day, her jet-black hair was tied up into a high bun coated with pork-lard to make her hair extra glossy and glistening. The high bun was also decorated with a lot of fresh flowers.

There were multiple matchmaker elderly women who acted as the wedding-night advisors to my mother, and they advised the young bride that she must lay down in bed with her new husband. My mother was very innocent but in great fear of this new stranger as her husband. The matchmakers came checking on my mother's hair every morning and found out that none of the flowers in her hair were destroyed. Her high bun was as fresh as on the wedding day. On the third morning after the wedding, the matchmakers filed a complaint to my grandmother that the new bride did not do as she was told.

My grandmother came to the wedding chamber and scolded the young bride for not allowing her husband to consummate the marriage. My mother was told that if she did not comply, she would end up being kicked out of her new in-law's luxurious fifty-room home and possibly be sent to a nunnery as damaged goods. The second alternative was to submit my mother as the seventh concubine for the rich seventy-year-old man in the Xiamen province near the sea. Being a concubine did not involve marriage because a concubine was a mere pleasure toy. The third option was to commit suicide by swallowing large quantity of opium, so the family name would not fall into disgrace.

Returning to my mother's old home was never an option because the Chinese believed that once a daughter was married, she was equivalent to a bucket of water that had been splashed outside the family front door. After all, the goat and pig from the dowry had long been slaughtered and consumed, and therefore there was not any way to make a U-turn in an arranged marriage.

With her limited options, on the fourth night, my mother obeyed and followed her mother's orders. Most importantly, to disobey a parent's order was equivalent to the height of disrespect and dishonor that would make ancestors turn in their graves. I am not sure whether there was love between my mother and my father at that stage, but sure enough, my mother started to give birth every nine months from then on.

Three years after the arranged marriage, three boys had been produced by my mother. Unfortunately, due to a harsh winter, my mother's second boy died from pneumonia when he was merely thirty days old. Decades after his death, my mom often talks about her second child, who was small but handsome like my father. Mom would often talk about his little rosy cheeks and pink lips, but he was lost most astonishingly due to malnutrition. Even at the age of ninety-eight, my mother's eyes often flowed with tears when she recalled her loss. That was the reason I lived in fear of disclosing my sickness to my mother when my prognosis was looking grim. The sadness of burying one's child must be the biggest curse in human history, and I always carry extra consideration for my mother. The last thing I wanted to do was to burden her with my challenges.

When the communist party took over China, my father's family was taken to the beach where the family business was located, and every single young man was shot to death in one ambush. No crime was committed, but I heard that my father's third brother was accused by the communist informers that he had been printing fake money, but this was a fabricated accusation. Even without this fictitious crime, the communist party believed being rich in those days was a crime in itself. The communist party had a little decency and spared my grandfather, who was an elderly man.

My father found out all his brothers were executed while he was out playing mahjong the night of the ambush. Without a chance to bid farewell, my father escaped the mahjong club in his simple but white underpants. My father borrowed a neighbor's bicycle to pedal to the nearest ship, leaving for Singapore that same night. The image of a young man escaping the barbarism of the Red China army on a bicycle has stuck in my head for many years, and I have the utmost admiration for my very quick-witted father.

Once again, my mother was abandoned to care for two young sons and an elderly father-in-law in the tumultuous days of Red China. My mom went to the beach, scooping up the shattered brains of her dead relatives while the communist party was not there. It was a windy night, and the tides were high, but my mother did not want her in laws' remains to be washed away by the sea. Collecting and assembling the whole bodies for the family was the honorable thing to do. Whenever my mother told me this story, she would recollect her brave attempt to recover the remains of her in-laws, and she considered this act merely a family obligation to honor the good name of the Loke family.

During the early communist days in China, my mother's fearlessness, and devotion to her in-laws as a young mother were beyond words. My paternal grandfather was an honorable man who appreciated my mother's ability to produce many grandsons. Even though my father's stepmother was very mean and abusive toward my mother, my grandfather always looked out for my mother while my father was separated from her. My father vowed to return to retrieve his wife, children, and father when he had gathered sufficient money.

During the forced separation, apart from restarting my father's business in Singapore, my father sought some comfort from other women while his wife and sons were held in China. Among all the sundry women my father became friends with, there was one particular girl that my father grew to be fond of. My father wrote to my grandfather and asked for his permission to officially admit this girl into the Loke family as my father's concubine. My grandfather was very protective of my mother, who had already delivered three grandsons to carry the Loke family name.

I understand communicating via handwritten letters was the only way of communication in those days given there was no telephone nor internet. My grandfather did write a strongly worded letter to reprimand my father for betraying my mother's devotion to the Loke family. Many years later, my father still kept that letter in his safety box made of cast iron. When I was a teenager, my father shared that letter with me and taught me the importance of familial obligation and commitment. Once my father received my grandfather's letter, there would be no more talk of acquiring a concubine ever again.

My mother would tell me this story multiple times, but somehow, I could not judge nor blame my father for his temporary disloyalty to my mother, given that the tradition of acquiring multiple concubines for a well-off family was a norm in those days. I am glad my father followed his father's order. Although I had never met my paternal grandfather, since he passed away while my mother was pregnant with me, after reading his letter to my father, I sensed that he was a man of great virtue and righteousness.

My father was a savvy businessman. He restarted his business by selling boiled peanuts in the developing country of Singapore. My father delivered boiled peanuts to customers on the bicycle he borrowed on the night he escaped the communists. Each peanut he sold became the hope to rescue his wife and family.

From selling boiled peanuts, my father expanded his business to trade raw coffee beans. My father's coffee business took off, and he became the king of importing and exporting coffee beans in the Southeast Asian area. When my father made enough money to buy three tickets for a one-way voyage from Fujian, China to Singapore, my father fulfilled his promise. After all the hard work and forced separation, there was a glimmer of hope for my father and mother to be reunited.

People of the village where my mother was residing heard the news of her traveling to Singapore, and a neighbor begged my mother to take her son on her behalf. When my mother was boarding the ship, the communist commander informed my mother that she could only travel with two children. Since my mother had promised to take care of her neighbor's son, her sense of responsibility told her to leave one of her sons behind safely with his grandfather and try and secure his travel later.

As the ship was departing, the communist commander heard about my mother's selfless act. He asked my mother to stop weeping, and my mom was allowed to board the ship with all three children. Finally, my mother was able to reunite with my father in Singapore after eight years of forced separation. My father did keep his promise, and the rest of my parents' life stories needs to be told in another book.

As can be seen, there were a million reasons why I could not bring my elderly mother another piece of sad news when I was confronted with my sickness. I never wanted my siblings to be burdened with the responsibilities of being the messenger of bad news. I pondered over and over how I could ease the message to my mother in person. I also believe that a mother has a right to know where her children are. The fact that my gang of siblings decided not to inform my mother regarding the death of my fourth brother, Richard, for over six years contributed to my anxiety about keeping secrets. How we covered up the facts for so many years was difficult for me to agree with, and I did not want to burden my loved ones by disguising my sickness from my mother any longer.

Though I was in the maintenance phase of my treatment, I still had to negotiate hard with my medical team for a three-week break and flew to Singapore to inform my mother in August 2022. Traveling was difficult because of the bone aches and joint pains but, nonetheless, I traveled safely to my hometown in Malaysia just across the causeway from Singapore.

My mother was in the intensive care unit when I arrived at her house. She was hospitalized for double pneumonia coupled with pulmonary edema (infectious fluids in the lungs). It was a touch-and-go situation for anyone, let alone someone so elderly, and I was afraid she might not survive this latest bout. Miraculously, my ninety-eight-year-old mother bounced back like a cat with nine lives after a few days of convalescing in the hospital.

After collecting my mother from the hospital, I was blessed with an uninterrupted two weeks of mother-daughter time. I was able to hold my mother's hands to calm her when she was sick. When my mother was conscious and well, I decided to show some of my bald-headed photographs as an icebreaker to my deliverance of cancer news. My very cute but senile mother laughed at my photographs and uttered that I was a stunning monk with my shaved head. My mom was a woman with a sense of humor. She thought that when visitors came to see her with masks during the pandemic, it was because these visitors did not like the smell of old people.

My mom relaxed me, and the laughter eased my way to inform her that I had been sick. Strangely enough and to my surprise, my mother was very pragmatic about my news. She took the information in a matter-of-fact manner and held my hand to say that I would be healed. My mother was an elderly woman who went through the Second World War, the emotional torture of being abandoned by her parents, the communist party's robbery of her young married life, the famine, and the Black Death in China. She was raised in fires and amid bullets, emerging as an enigma shrouded with strength. I used to say to myself that when I grew up, I wanted to be just like my mother because she had been the perfect example of resilience.

Being able to converse with my mom in person about my health challenges was an enormous mental relief because keeping a familial secret was not a skill, I was good at nor indeed one that I wanted to be good at. I longed to tell my mother all the details, but I was not sure if at her age, she had the cognitive ability to comprehend what facing cancer entailed. Nonetheless, my second wish from my genie was fulfilled, and I felt the stress of keeping a secret from my parent simply melt away.

Additionally, to be able to discuss my sickness with my mother, I also benefited from some tranquil and eventful nights with her. It was the rainy season when I visited Malaysia, and the tropical rains were often followed by vicious mosquitoes. I was able to set up a spare bed next to my mother and conquered those pesky insects while she was too weak to swat them away. My mother also had the habit of being active at night due to her sundown dementia. I was able to guard her by myself while watching her somewhat entertaining activities in the dead of night. Mother would demonstrate a sudden surge of energy when no one was watching her. Just like a dog or a cat with the "zoomies," she would become as strong as the Incredible Hulk, often in the small hours of the morning.

I learned from my elderly mother how important it was to surround oneself with family members who truly love one another. The mere act of stroking my mother's hands while she was in peaceful slumber is something I will always treasure.

My mother never intended to depend on others for her day-to-day functioning. Her survival instincts taught her to bounce back after multiple incidents of hospitalization. If I am not mistaken, she has survived multiple pulmonary edemas, pneumonia, and high blood pressure. One cannot help but admire this cat with nine lives, and she has truly taught me the meaning of survivorship.

Chapter Eighteen

The Child
Bride with
an Abandonment
Wound

"I can't cry because I need to survive." – Unknown

I have always wanted to write a book about my mother and father. My parents were the products of 1920s China, going through various chapters of the Chinese Revolution, communist mayhem, and all sorts of political turmoil. In a prior chapter, I gave a short review of my mother's life, but in truth I have mentally written a large book about my mother because there are endless stories I have heard that are worth retelling. That book was written a hundred times but rewritten a thousand. The primary reason for not completing the book on my parents was because I had yet to organize my thoughts so that I would not favor one parent over the other. The second reason, of course, was because my cancer interrupted my life ever so slightly.

My mother, the Yoda of survivorship and my maestro of resilience, has dedicated her life to be a good daughter, wife, and parent. She has my utmost respect and love. I grew up looking up at my mother's face, greedily consuming up all the adventures and stories that she told me. My mother is a great storyteller, and if she were able to write, her books would be classics.

My mother has difficulty trusting anyone due to her complex personalities entwined with her childhood abandonment scars. Her self-confidence is lacking, and she has minimal trust with anyone outside of her children. The sense of betrayal from her birth parents has had a lingering impact on her life, where she feels she cannot rely on anyone. Since my mother is now approaching ninety-nine years of age and dementia is starting to appear, sometimes, her storytelling becomes even more vivid and packed full of imagination and exaggeration.

My cancer-induced anxiety did not stem from my mom's lack of trust with anyone; instead, my apprehension originated from my inability to hide the truth from my parents. Even being economic with the truth, I believe, is a form of lying.

My habit of telling all is due to a very memorable incident when I was a mere four-year-old girl. While playing rough with my three brothers, I accidentally knocked over my father's favorite lookalike Ming vase. I decided to go to my father and confess. Instead of being scolded, my father held my hand and told me because of my honesty and that I was brave enough to tell the truth, there would still be dinner for me that night and no punishment was necessary. This loving way of handling a child's confession served me well, and I would never intentionally hide any secrets from my parents.

When I was young, I used to play hard and rough with three of my brothers who were closer to my age. I was definitely well-known for my tomboyish behaviors and bravery, and my father often said to me that I would have been perfect if I had been born a boy. My parents were Asian; it was, and in some cases still is, an ancient perception that boys are more practical and useful in the family.

My mother told me that on the day I was born, my father arrived at the hospital excited to see yet another baby boy. When the nurse told my father that I turned out to be a healthy young baby girl, my father swiftly turned around and slammed the door of his Mercedes-Benz and left with a huff, without visiting me or my mother. I am not entirely sure this story is factually accurate, but I have to take my mom's words as real. The implicit memories of her own abandonment were reactivated. This had no real impact on me though.

When my mother and I were discharged from the maternity ward, my father came to collect us in his Mercedes-Benz. While my mother was holding me in her arms sitting in the back seat, my father apparently suggested to my mother that I should be gifted to his cousin who lived in Penang (Northern Malaysia) since his cousin longed to have a daughter of his own but was unable to. Penang is some ten hours' drive from my hometown. My mother shed a few tears without responding to my father. My father noticed my mother's sadness via his rear-view mirror and never raised the subject again.

I mentioned earlier that my mother was triggered since she was given away without any explanation by her biological parents. My father appeared to be ambivalent around my mother's feelings on the topic of adoption and abandonment. That was when my mother put her foot down and defied her husband's wish. From that day on, my father knew that this number ten, perfectly-formed child – me – would not leave his arms because he had hurt my mom's feelings.

When we arrived at home, my father decided to name me "beautiful and perfect," and that was how my father perceived me throughout my life.

My mother has recounted this story to me many times, and I have grown to believe this incident must be true. Since I became a mother myself, I know that the bond between a mother and a daughter is the most unique attachment in humankind. When I was an expectant mother, I felt the little hiccough when baby Gigi was in my womb and loved every hiccough she had. I thought her hiccough was like Gigi sending a little message to tell me that she was all right and very comfortable. Every little kick felt like an affirmation that the baby wanted to hang around with the mother as long as she could.

Although I am not responsible for my mother's abandonment wounds, I lived vicariously around her feelings. My mother has severe separation anxiety to the extent that she will often complain that none of her children ever come to visit her. Even when my second sister had just spent four months living with her, my mother will conveniently forget that my sister was there.

Scientists claim that all babies have the primal instinct to bond with their biological mother, to become acquainted with her smell, voice, feelings, and taste during the nine-month gestation period. Being given away for adoption is to remove a child's primordial sense of comfort and safety. When my mother lost her sense of safety, her survival instincts grew stronger and stronger.

My father, on the other hand, lived a contented childhood until the village he lived in encountered the equivalent of the Black Death caused by plague-infested rats. Within seven days, my father's seven biological brothers and his mother had passed away due to the plague. I remember when I was a small child at home, whenever my father heard that there was a sighting of a mouse or a rat, my father would jump on the table out of fear. I guess that event cast a dark mental image on my father.

My father was only six years old and had to endure the sudden loss but was blessed with one remaining member of his family: his father. My grandfather was still a young man, and he remarried. However, my father's new mother was not a pleasant stepmother, according to my mother. My father often hid himself at other people's house or mahjong clubs in China in order to avoid his stepmother's whipping broomstick. After the stepmother delivered two new stepbrothers, my father's position at home became untenable. With his stepmother's thrashings as part of his upbringing, my father also learned to survive and became a very shrewd businessman. I recall my father told me how he learned to grease the family heavy wooden doors with pork lard and cotton balls to avoid making sounds of escape, so he would sneak out of the house at night to avoid being beaten if found out.

In recalling my parents' survivor stories, I would hypothesize that my strong survival instinct and skills emanated from my ancestors, who evolved in harsh settings. Spending time and learning from my parents has enriched my life skills, and I thank my parents for helping to get me through my cancer journey.

Chapter Nineteen

You Will Never See a U-Haul Behind a Hearse

"Letting go gives us freedom, and freedom is the only condition for happiness." – Nhat Hanh

On February 7, 2023, I flew to Houston for my end-of-treatment scans and bloodwork. By that time, I was traveling by myself, and catching an Uber was my usual mode of transportation from Houston Intercontinental Airport to MD Anderson. It was a beautiful sunny morning with the customary bumper-to-bumper traffic on the way into the city.

Making customary small talk with my Uber driver was a reaffirmation of the kindness of strangers. He was very sympathetic, as if it was his first time driving a cancer patient to MD Anderson. He turned his head while the traffic was at a standstill and said to me, "God will take care of you."

At that moment, even sitting in Houston traffic became a joy. I wanted to sing out loud, and so I turned on my Apple Music and started to play Sam Cooke's gospel song, "Touch the Hem of His Garment." The driver and I sang alongside Sam Cooke at the top of our lungs, like so: "Whoa, there was a woman in the Bible days. She has been sick, sick so very long…" It gave me a lot of hope to have this Muslim man and me both singing a Christian song at the top of our lungs.

I am a Christian but not particularly religious, so singing gospel music in an Uber along the Houston highway was never something I could have imagined doing. At all times during my treatment, I have felt lucky and blessed. Too few people are protected by a Cadillac private health insurance plan that covered me all the way. My mind started to recap some of the life experiences that took place while I was in Houston eagerly seeking to touch the hem of His garment.

Unlike some cancer patients, I never elected to ring the bell, i.e., a traditional expression of freedom when the treatment is over. There were three main reasons for this. First, celebrating by ringing the bell might awaken my nemesis, Toby. Second, who is to state that Toby will never return given all the doctoral and scientific research papers I read? At the beginning of the journey, I actively sought out the bells at MD Anderson, curious to see how big they were and where they were located. I found them, but then decided not to ring them. Third, I also felt guilty that perhaps ringing such a bell in a ward full of cancer patients who were still gathering their strength to fight their wars was insensitive. I didn't feel the desire to brag about the end of my treatment because of the three Rs of cancer: it has a habit of being relentless, recalcitrant, and recurring.

The Houston traffic was particularly heavy that morning. When Sam Cooke's song came to an end, I looked out the windows and realized there were many beautiful things in life that I never truly appreciated. The baby-blue sky was decorated with fluffy white clouds like innocent angels spreading their wings above me. The sturdy and giant Houston skyline elevated my mood, as if they were all standing behind me, giving me the best applause and support. I realized all the little things in life did spark joy for me. The fact that a mother deer had chosen to use my front lawn as a maternity ward to give birth to her fawns should have brought a smile to my face, but I had always taken it for granted. The fact that my senile old housecat loved chasing her tail in the kitchen was also a little thing that should have brightened my life. Whoever said *don't sweat the small stuff* was right, but the quote should be about loving and appreciating all the little things in life.

Looking out of the window to my left, I saw a long black hearse transporting an individual who had departed this world. Strangely enough, I did not see a U-Haul being towed behind it. I then remembered the quote that "We all came into this world naked, and the rest is all a drag." I had an epiphany that the most burdensome objects that we carry are our thoughts and mindset; a large diamond ring wasn't much use when on a breathing tube trying to cherish the last moment of being alive.

As I sat in that solid traffic jam, I started to run down the list of things that I did not need and the time I did not have to waste. The conclusion was that I should appreciate all things but not necessarily sweat about all things. I became relaxed and unrestricted, and my mind began to wonder what it would be like to be free of cancer treatment.

Finally, we arrived at the cancer center. I donated my usual three vials of fresh blood for testing, eagerly waiting for my end-of-treatment CT scan. The very next day, when the CT scan results became available, Dr. Westin gave me the great news that I was officially in remission, and she did not need to see me for the next three months.

I also met with Dr. Klopp, who congratulated me. I believe the consummate teamwork at MD Anderson was the difference and the key ingredient to my success in fighting Toby and Tory. At that point, I believed even my Lord was brokenhearted and decided to restore my broken spirit.

MD Anderson and I commenced the battle burdened with millions of unknowns twenty months prior, and the outcome had not been in my control. The only thing in my prayerful hands was my faith in the medical team, and all I knew was to stay the course. As Stephen Covey said, "I am not a product of my circumstances. I am a product of my decisions." I reminded myself that life is about five percent what happens to me and ninety-five percent how I react to what happens to me. I applauded my family for giving me the strength and resources to relocate to Houston followed by twelve months of flying to Houston every three weeks for my maintenance infusions. We were on top of that challenge, and the hard work had paid off.

Just like a caged bird set free, I began the discussion with my lead oncologist as to how soon we could remove my chemotherapy port. Having to live with the chemotherapy port during the treatment had made me self-conscious, and I was always trying to disguise the port with scarves and extra clothing. The PA and nurses gave me the standard advice that a patient in remission normally had to keep the port in situ for another year just in case the same cancer revisited. I knew I was not the type of pessimistic person who would elect to live with a foreign object implanted just to allow Toby or his offspring to re-invade my body. The chemo port was as obvious as a white cue ball on a pool table, which I sarcastically referred to as my third nipple. It symbolized and branded me as a cancer patient for nearly two years, and I was not willing to keep it for any longer than needed.

I advocated for myself and reached an agreement with my medical team, who said the port would be surgically removed within three months starting from the day of my remission notification. Being categorized as a cancer patient whenever a stranger stared at my port was an uncomfortable experience. Nobody likes to be pigeonholed or adversely discriminated against when living with chemotherapy infusions.

I remember my journey back to Chicago from Houston after the remission news. The feeling of freedom was the likes of which I had never experienced before. I was not the kind of bird to be caged, but the twenty months of treatment sure felt like some kind of imprisonment.

One of my favorite statues at MD Anderson is the bronze sculpture of a young lady setting a bird free from her hands. Below this statue is the famous quote by Victor Hugo that goes like this: "Be like the bird that, passing on her flight awhile on boughs too slight, feels them give way beneath her, and yet sings, knowing how she hath wings."

In those two years, whenever the boughs beneath me felt like giving way, I was secure in the knowledge that MD Anderson's wings were there to support me.

During all those trips to Houston, I always made a point of paying my respects to that particular bronze statute. I longed to be set free with every single cell in my body. That day of remission news reminded me of what freedom smelt and felt like. I knew my wings would take flight again given the expertise of the medical team. I did not worry about what would happen to me next because my injured wings were repaired.

Chapter Twenty

In Retrospect

"The real trick in life is to turn hindsight into foresight that reveals insight." – Robin Sharma

Many of my family members and friends had questioned why I had a tumor the size of Texas and was oblivious to its existence for so long. I do not want to sound like a dejected individual who was stuck in the past and marinating in a victim mentality; however, I need to take a retrospective look.

My cancer was called clear cell carcinoma, and it originated from my uterus. Endometrial (uterine or corpus) cancers can present themselves early by exhibiting symptoms of abnormal uterine bleeding or spotting. This kind of bleeding has no pain and can be mistaken for menstruation. I never had bleeding until the day before I found out I had cancer, so Toby was sneaky and devious – as are many of his relatives. I had slight abdominal pain regularly especially after a meal followed by a bloating sensation, as if I had overeaten even when I had only consumed a small amount of food. Outside of mealtimes, I often felt pelvic pressure.

During Thanksgiving, the year before my diagnosis, while friends and family gathered, someone commented that I had lost a lot of weight. I am diabetic, and weight loss very often was explained away by my medication. Simultaneously, I was on a low-carb diet to manage my blood glucose. So, my reaction to the weight comments was that my low-carb lifestyle must have worked. I did not take note of the weight loss nor placed any significance on my friend's observation.

Going back further, mid-summer before my illness, I woke up with two of my little toes on my left foot swollen like the red nose of Rudolph the reindeer. It was at the start of the unknown territory of COVID-19, so I had a Zoom consultation with my general practice doctor. The swollen toes presented themselves with zero warning. My doctor concluded it was gout on my left foot. After two doses of gout medications, the swelling did not improve. Reluctantly, I went for an X-ray and ultrasound to establish whether there was any structural damage to my toes, and the conclusion was there was not.

The swollen toes continued to vacation with me for a good six months. Meanwhile, I started to have severe hives consistently on my back every night after dinner. I went to visit three dermatologists, and all of them prescribed antihistamine cream and Benadryl tablets. During the holiday season, I began to suffer from bowel obstructions and was seeking a gastrointestinal expert thinking I had issues in that area. I have to admit, before my cancer diagnosis, I was always reluctant to visit doctors, thinking I could just adjust my diet and lifestyle to adjust as necessary.

The lessons learned from this chapter are to *listen to and hear* your body. When my health was in jeopardy, it did exhibit signs of illness, but I chose to dismiss them. I was prioritizing work above my health ,and hence I was in a state of denial that I would ever get sick. I was not a good listener of my own body. I tried to listen, but I did not hear. The realization point came when I faced the fear of a painful death from cancer.

The second lesson learned was that a woman's yearly wellness checkup does not always detect ovarian or endometrial cancers. The general perception from a lot of innocent women was that my doctor gave me my negative pap smear result, so I must be healthy. The reality is that a woman's pelvic health can be distorted by misconceived yearly checkups. Pelvic area cancers can be silent and devious, in my experience, and I did not show signs of endometrial bleeding until the day before my diagnosis. In retrospect, Toby really did not play fair nor gave me any heads up. Stupidity was my middle name, and before I knew it, I had let Toby violate me below the belt, so to speak.

Chapter Twenty-One

Motto to Live By

"Hindsight provides new eyes." – *Wayne Dyer*

Life is not a journey to our final resting place in an immaculate body dressed in our finest. I would like to believe that, as someone once said, I would arrive at my funeral skidding in sideways and covered in bruises, scars, and brown dirt. I wish for Gigi to dress up as Shrek and Keith as Princess Fiona, humming the tune of "Hallelujah" as my coffin slides into the furnace – but not yet.

Scratches and bumps are part of what has made me wiser in life. If a person never falls, how will they learn how not to fall? Cancer winners are not individuals who never fell but people who never quit. As the equestrians say, a good rider has to fall off their horses two hundred times to become an exemplary rider. Each time Mohammed Ali took punches, he learned how to avoid the next hit by floating like a butterfly. I was a die-hard equestrian and a boxer before my diagnosis, and I often wondered whether I was born tough or trained myself to be tough. One thing is for sure: I never deem myself a loser in life when I fail in my experiments; instead, I merely become wiser.

I do not claim to be a life coach or a pundit of spirituality. The techniques I list below are not a mantra nor a holy pilgrimage. However, these are a few principles that worked for me:-

- Always look on the bright side of life – Eric Idle in *Monty Python*.

- Love oneself profusely, and always be my own advocate.

- Appreciate all those who help me in life.

- Never burden my loved ones with my sickness.

- Always think outside the box.

- Health comes before wealth.

- Do not let cancer steal my joy.

- Loving my scars from adventure.

- Surround oneself with positive people.

- Avoid self-pity.

Imagine lying in a bluebell field and wishing every bluebell belongs to you. While you are busy collecting all the bluebells, you forget to lie on the field to enjoy the sunshine beating down on your face. My neighbor has a bluebell field in front of his house and each spring, his whole front yard is a magical sea of boundless blue blooms. If I was on this bluebell field, I would lay myself flat marinating in the sun, thinking to myself while I am there admiring the view, there are plenty of us that have departed and are now chewing bluebells by the roots from below. I do not have to work so hard to pick all the bluebells; I merely have to lie down and pick whatever bluebells I can reach and would be contented with just a few.

Happiness is exclusively and wholly self-defined, so I never let others tell me how to be happy or when or where to be happy. If making snow angels among the bluebells makes me happy, so be it. Who is to judge except me? Making snow angels in a bed of flowers is not the same as in the snow – for my life has been all about thinking outside the box and living wholeheartedly with a constant paradigm shift. I have decided that I will knock on my neighbor's door this coming spring so I might roll on his acres of bluebells like a toddler without any reservation because that would be happiness as defined by me.

There is a key difference between success and happiness. As Dale Carnegie said, "Success is getting what you want. Happiness is wanting what you get." I saw a photograph of a group of young kids in India holding up one of their flip-flops to simulate a smartphone for selfies. The smiles on their faces while simulating the selfie were the most innocent but gratifying version of a smile. This image touched me so deeply, and I realized I do not have to go chasing butterflies. I merely have to sit on a field of dandelions, and the butterflies will land on my knee while I meditate. I no longer aspire for more Gucci bags or Versace dresses or Cartier jewelry, because going about my daily life without the burden of any belongings is a much more pleasing existence.

As a toddler, I knew how to generate unbridled happiness, such as blowing the seeds off dandelions. I made wishes on those seeds, which I imagined were a fairy godmother's magic powder. After my life of Toby and Tory, I re-ignited that childlike innocence and imagination, and I was able to fabricate my version of happiness without any boundaries or filters. Growing up in a less prosperous country, I did not need fancy computer games to keep me happy; just keeping a gold spider in a little matchbox was a joy to me then. Collecting fireflies in a mason jar was purposeful and blissful. Playing jump rope and flying kites kept me entertained and contented. Our designer shoes were simple flip-flops or wooden clogs made out of hollowed-out coffin wood.

When my body was going through pain, I turned each teardrop into pearls of wisdom. I once said to my sister, who was with me during my treatment, "How could I complain about cancer pains when Jesus died for us on the cross?"

She understood what I meant because not only did I have faith in my medical team, but I also always blanketed myself with emotional sustenance from the faith of the force high above. Previously, I liked to think that I was a scientist and hence was not very religious. However, when faith in the medical team cannot fulfill the needs of complete mental healing, you have to reach up to a higher level. I did hear about the sickly woman in the Bible days, and, as I indicated, I could relate to the story of the woman who touched the hem of His garment.

When friends asked how I handled my illness, I told them there were only three important ingredients to my survival. First was the love and support from my family and friends, second was my relentless survivor instincts, last but not least was faith. Faith could take on many shapes and forms. I prayed to God, Allah, Buddha, the Hindu gods, etc. that are trusted by many. Going to public places for prayer was not a done thing during the pandemic, but there were so many friends who prayed for me via Zoom meetings in my gloomiest moments. I even used a singing bowl from Tibet with incense gifted to me by a girlfriend of mine who recommended I try meditation. The love from these friends safeguarded me through the treatment and beyond.

Receiving all this support made me want to make my life more alive than ever.

Once my treatment was over, I felt like a phoenix rising from the ashes and discovering its' rebirth. I could not begin to draft this memoir until all my treatments were complete simply because I did not know how my story was going to end. When I was informed that I was in remission, I concluded that suffering would, in fact, lead to salvation. I accepted my suffering as a gift from above. Jokingly, I would say that I was sent to the university of hard knocks, but I came out as a graduate feeling much more educated and accomplished. Simultaneously, I no longer wanted to sit in the passenger seat of life. As far as the search for happiness, I wanted to be the captain and take the wheel so I might find my true happiness again.

Surviving Toby made me reevaluate my lifestyle, diet, and habits. It was also pointless attempting to return to the person I used to be. The day I heard my remission news was the day I placed a sturdy lid in my genie bottle to securely contain previous versions of me. I might want to peek in the bottle from time to time to reference the former me; however, the genuine intention was to seal this lid once and for all.

I had spent three and a half years researching the correlation between emotional intelligence and workplace resistance to change, which was published as part of my Ph.D. That day was the day I embraced what I researched and began to love the new changes in my personal life. The difference between the words *change* and *chance* is just one letter.

Toby was a change that I converted into a chance. Where other people saw cancer as a difficulty, I saw it as an opportunity to thrive. Who would deny me the desire to embrace my new lifestyle of daily exercise, eating lots of vegetables, and drinking lots of pomegranate juice? Going to detox in my sauna and steam room before soaking in a bubble bath became a part of my daily routine. I took time for self-love, and I took time to allow my body to recover. There was no longer a five a.m. wake-up call to disturb my slumber. If I overslept, the world wasn't going to end. The only way I want to be woken up from now on is the chirping of summer birds flapping around my twelve linden trees in the front yard.

I re-learned how to appreciate nature. On my daily walk, I purposely hunted for wild mushrooms to study them. Mushrooms are the most ancient survivors on planet Earth. I was curious and wanted to learn how mushrooms could outlast dinosaurs and survive to thrive. I became a self-discovered mycologist. I would photograph these wild mushrooms to study them and realize they were survivors because they lived simply on rotten wood, dead insects, water, and fresh air. Nature did not only heal my soul, but it also helped me get closer to who I was. Every day I would check these wild mushrooms, which had a habit of transforming as and when their surroundings changed. Being able to adapt and embrace life's new challenges was an essential ingredient for survival.

In my adventure, I began to appreciate what Mahatma Gandhi meant when he said, "There is more to life than increasing its speed." I slowed down and stopped being the busy sock-stealer of the family and began to notice what things sparked joy for me. Flexing my polychronicity by overachieving at work often caused me to lose my focus on being a good daughter, an attentive wife, and an involved mother. Before my diagnosis, I always pushed myself to work two hundred percent harder than the next colleague. I am not even sure what I was trying to prove since I was already a very successful businessperson who had accomplished a lot.

I also elected to surround myself with positive people who knew that I would come out of the other end not just as a survivor but as a winner. My philosophy is that if there are more tears than smiles in the room, then leave the room. The ocean of cancer has always been packed full of sorrowful stories and despondent people. For me, to thrive and aim for a positive outcome, it was best not to actively seek out fellow cancer warriors. Whilst listening and affording survivor skills to comrades of the disease is a nice gesture, it can often drag one into a swirl of sadness and hopelessness. Fighting Toby and Tory was as much a medical as a mental game. If I had walked into the infusion or radiation sessions burdened with others' situations, it would have pulled me further down the lane of self-pity.

Self-pity is a warrior's worst enemy. I try not to give in to low self-esteem or unnecessary benevolence to myself or fellow cancer fighters while trying to avoid being hard-hearted. Self-pity often destroys relationships and is a disservice to your loved ones who try to care for you. I believe it can hurt a cancer patient. Never did I ask the "why me?" question to my God, my loved ones, or my medical team. Instead, I tried to ask the question, "Why not me?" I told myself these were the cards that were dealt to me, so I was going to play those cards with intelligence and logical actions.

Just before my diagnosis, I completed my Ph.D. dissertation by researching the area of emotional intelligence for absorbing life changes. Never in my wildest dreams did I think that I would have to draw on my academic research to assist me in my emotion perception and utilization to deal with my situation.

I recall when visiting my friend, who was struck by a more deadly cancer six years ago, there was constant bitterness and the "why me?" question before his final days. It saddened me greatly to hear the grief and stress he imposed on himself and his caregivers. I learned from his journey that thou shall not burden one's loved ones, who clearly cannot assist in answering the "why me" question and hence, I accepted my situation as given. On the flip side, I never let Toby or Tory inconvenience my life. I once stated that Toby and Tory were merely a dropped stitch in the tapestry of life (thanks, David Jason), and I was never going to let cancer be the main topic during our treatment periods.

Instead, Keith and I chose to spend our time meaningfully. We went to various outdoor music concerts and traveled to my hometown in Malaysia when I was strong enough to fly long distances. We still dined at some fine dining restaurants, but we showed up in T-shirts and jeans. I turned off my work computer for a solid twenty months and shut off my work emails completely and focused on living well. As a matter of fact, I checked out of the workforce and have forgotten my passwords, and I consider that a major accomplishment.

As an almost-sexagenarian, I had learned to curtail physical activities to avoid unnecessary injuries. Life before blood thinners, I was an active boxer and equestrian. I had no hesitation in jabbing my husband via a sport called fencing – the only legal manner to neutralize my daily frustration without killing each other. Fencing is a combat sport featuring three different disciplines known as the foil, the épée, and the saber. I yearned for physical torture to pump up my endorphins like a long-distance runner does. I enjoyed honing my épée skills. In addition, arduous gym workouts were the rhythm of my life to cope with my empty-nest depression.

Life after Toby made me appreciate much simpler things in life, such as walking. Walking was often the under-appreciated gift that I missed. My good friend, Dr. Brad, who is an orthopedic surgeon, always advocated walking as the best medicine. When a person chooses to live life in the fast lane, walking doesn't seem productive enough because it is the slowest mode of transport. When I remember the day I could not walk even two steps from the parked car to the curb and we had to turn the car right back to go home, my perspective changed. I often pinch myself, as if I am dreaming now that I can walk for at least three miles a day. Walking prevents blood clots but also buoys your mood. I formed my ideas for this book many times during my recovery walks, and the content of this book was framed in my head during my miles and miles of gentle strides. Naturalists and hikers often say that after a long walk in the forest, they feel taller than the trees. Walking was becoming the most meaningful way to spend my time. Just like Forrest Gump, I became known as a frequent walker in my village.

Chapter Twenty-Two

Lady on a Harley and the Flying Soup

" *A friend is someone who knows all about you and still loves you.*" *- Elbert Hubbard*

The day after I received my remission verdict, I received a personal phone call from my rheumatologists that one of my blood test results might have been abnormal. Abnormal, as in a certain protein serum was very high and required further investigation. I was asked to give some blood samples for more specific tests for potential myeloma, another form of cancer, with the assumption that the various bone and muscle aches I was complaining about might need some illumination.

Given a person with a cancer history, a responsible medical team would always take all kinds of precautions to avoid the return of the cancer cells or the potential brewing of new forms of cancer. I was anxious to hear the suspected new disease. However, I concurred the extra due diligence my medical team took.

After giving a second batch of blood for a retest and new protein tests, I was somewhat exhausted and emotionally drained. Never did I ask the "Why me?" question during the battle, but I started to ponder what else could be lurking in my body that was going to jump out of the bush like Chucky from the thriller slasher movie. Worrying about the cancer's revisit is most intense during the first year of remission. Cancer recurrence can be a fact of life, and recurrence fear is as normal as teenagers fearing dating after a brutal breakup.

As resilient as I was, there came to a point in the boxing match where I needed a drink to regroup myself. I texted a girlfriend of mine, Dr. Emma, who happened to be a Ph.D. in chemistry, a practicing lawyer, an equestrian, and a professional Pilates trainer. Dr. Emma owns a rose pink and immaculate Pilates reformer equipment, which warranted her the title of the Lady on a Harley. In addition to the pink Harley, she possesses numerous Pilates apparatus which would make Joseph Hubertus Pilates proud.

I was a complete newcomer to the mind-body Contrology world of Pilates and was intimidated by the reformer and transformer equipment. They reminded me of a medieval torture chamber coupled with *Fifty Shades of Grey*. During my treatment, Dr. Emma gently introduced me to various relaxation activities to help me through the pain. She was a busy lady, but she took time out and gave me her undivided attention in all aspects, both physically and mentally. I was blessed to have numerous private lessons to help my somewhat damaged back due to poor posture from months of hunching over with pelvic pain.

Not to make any excuses, but my posture was certainly impaired during the treatment by bending inwards shaped like a croissant carrying a question mark due to pelvic area tightness and soreness. Knowing I was not physically capable of stretching or heavy gym work, Dr. Emma would surreptitiously arrange for me to join her in the spa for a salt-room, detoxing foot bath, and a long walk. Knowing I was complete with my chemical treatment, she took charge and became my personal Pilates advisor. At times when there were tears, she would whip out a light version of a good read from her church to redirect my negative mindset. Friends who were intelligent and were able to do subtle things to float me around the cancer rivers and oceans were individuals deserving of my undying gratitude.

Keith and I have been friends with Jean and Brad for the past twenty-four years. Our children shared the same interests in all things equestrian, and I had witnessed Jean and Brad's three young kids climbing our sixty-five-foot-tall linden trees when they were little. Exactly twelve linden trees embellished the hills of our front yard, and hence the neighbors referred to our property as Linden Hills. Linden Hills was the best childhood hiding place if tree-climbing was the thing you fancied as a young child.

In the summer, memories of the three young girls – Celine, Mary, and Gigi – swinging on the horse fences in my backyard attempting to bareback the ponies were priceless. On snowy winter nights, the girls would whip out the short and well-nourished grey pony named Hunter. The girls would take turns barebacking and cantering in our backyard in the knee-high snow under the moonlight. These and countless other memories of our children formed a solid foundation for our friendship.

Dr. Jean was a marvelous gourmet chef, and instead of sharing DIY tools, Keith and Jean would share recipes they eagerly collected from the internet. I did not cook, nor should I since I had friends who were constantly feeding me amazing homemade dishes. My daughter loved Jean's cooking so much, and she often told me her raison d'être for coming home for Thanksgiving was Jean's killer dishes. So many times, when the kids were growing up together, Jean had us at her dining table to savor her exceptional culinary skills.

During my stay in Houston, Keith was somewhat concerned about my loss of appetite and shared his worry with Dr. Jean. In a very strange way, having your husband discussing your weight might be an awkward conversation, but not for Keith and Dr. Jean.

Jean is a doctor with the heart of Mother Teresa. Not wanting to bear the image of my skinny bones, she got creative. She ordered a large tub of chicken and noodles soup supplemented with some homemade bread rolls to our apartment some one thousand and two hundred miles away. The soup was one of the few things I could keep down at that point. Twenty months later, I can still taste the love in the soup. Sometimes, little things friends do for one another are the most touching act, and writing this story still brings tears to my eyes.

Jean and Brad never ceased caring about Keith, Gigi, and me. The Jean and Brad family would be there to drink champagne with us when times were great and would also be there for us if our house was struck by lightning. True friends were those who actively marched on in my life when others left my world as soon as adversity struck.

Keith and I live on a beautiful farm in the suburbs of Chicago, and, despite the harsh winter, we have opted to stay here because there are always beautiful days of spring, summer, and autumn. The trees are always beautiful in gold, yellow, and red during the fall, and these are the scenes that money cannot buy.

When I was in Houston, I did miss walking around our street, enchanted by gorgeous fall colors. A dear friend of mine knew how badly I missed our farm. She took the trouble of driving down our street with her camera in one hand and steering her large truck with the other. A video of my well-missed home was sent to me, it warmed my heart to have just that small taste of home. Hard to explain, but the little things good friends did for me during my sick days were so precious and noteworthy.

When I was in Houston, I did have two friends who happened to reside in Texas. Given the size of the state, one of them would have to drive five hours just to visit me, and the other would have a drive of around eight hours. Nonetheless, I received those friends cheerfully during treatment. They loved me when I was not sick, but they loved me even more when I was poorly. Some friends surreptitiously mailed me meditation paraphernalia and calming tea and herbs. There was a friend who took Keith, Gigi, and me to her favorite Mexican restaurant and supplied me with drinks with no name. Unfortunately, being a rare drinker, I was so well-oiled that I vomited most of my dinner on the flower bushes in the back of her restaurant. I was afraid to show my face ever again in that somewhat scrumptious restaurant.

Dr. Rhianna is a dear friend of mine. Our daughters went to the same ballet school when they were just out of their diapers. She is a smart equestrian veterinarian who, similar to me, is very young at heart. She would visit me in Houston and use her magic hands to adjust my neck and back because she believes any creature that moves should have their posture corrected. Dr. Rhianna enjoyed various stopovers at our Linden Hills farm to see our horses and to adjust my daughter's elderly cat, Onkyo.

Most importantly, she has a great way of behaving like a young child because she will climb our tall linden trees whenever she visits. For a nearly sixty-year-old person on a high dosage of blood thinner medication, climbing trees might not be the recommended medical therapy for me. Nonetheless, I promise tree-climbing will be our next excursion when she returns to Linden Hills.

Chapter Twenty-Three

Healing

"*Our wounds are often the openings into the best and most beautiful part of us.*" – *David Richo*

Someone said time heals all wounds, but I cannot concur with this hypothesis. Time may lessen the memories of the adversity, but time does not make cancer scars disappear. Cancer patients long to hear the terms such as *no evidence of disease* (NED) or *remission*. After hearing those terms, cancer patients will long for the word *cured*. A person recovering from cancer very often will have the nightmare of the cancer returning. The wounds from cancer surgery often remain, and scars have an inexplicable authority of reminding us of our past.

The reality to face is that healing can take time. Our sense of well-being will depend on our lifestyle, diet, degree of stress, and amount of rest. I also remind myself that every day might not be perfect; however, there is something good in every day if I choose to seek it out. I am also ready to wash away all the debris from my cancerous past.

In the cancer recovery world, patients are categorized from "cancer patients" to "persons with a history of cancer." Cancer survivors are also catalogued as "early survivors" and "long-time survivors". I have a friend who is a breast cancer survivor, Brooklynn. She is ten years younger than me but completed her main cancer treatment some four years ago.

Brooklynn recalled the day her oncologist told her that she did not need more chemotherapy because the medical team could not find evidence of the disease (NED) which was confirmed when her scans could not locate the original tumor anymore. I joked with her that she should be elated since even Google could not find her old tumor. In contrast, Brooklynn told me she was very sad and felt abandoned and went back to beg for more chemotherapy. She was so afraid that the scans were mistaken, and she felt her security blanket for her ongoing treatment was removed.

I also briefly enquired about one of my friends, Frank, who had lung cancer. Frank was a heavy smoker and was diagnosed with late-stage lung cancer which had metastasized. All cancers have the potential to spread beyond its origin. Once the cancerous cells travel into the lymph nodes, there is a high chance that the disease would tour other parts of the body. Frank has been in remission for more than twelve years, but he told me his eyes are always on the ball, and he refuses to accept that he was completely cured.

I have another friend, Ariana, whose mother had the same cancer as me: clear cell carcinoma. Ariana's mother is now in her eighties. She fought her cancer in four separate bouts but survived. Her attitude appears to be determined and unwavering. Despite multiple surgeries to combat her disease, she remains upbeat and buoyant. This resilient cancer winner became my idol. I have adopted her optimistic outlook, diluted with a bit of Frank's *eyes on the ball* philosophy, and Toby and Tory remain on my surveillance radar.

Daily exercise improved my speed of recovery. I focused on making my days active by avoiding sedentary hobbies such as watching endless movies or playing board games. I enjoy reading, but to avoid being stagnant, I switched to audiobooks that allow me to be actively walking on a treadmill or pedaling an exercise bike. The benefit of listening to a book is minimizing screen time or eye strain from excessive reading.

As a cancer survivor, I no longer allow myself to do whatever I want or eat whatever I fancy. I grow my fresh and organic vegetables and avoid commercially grown produce with pesticides as much as possible. For relaxation, I use a sauna, steam room, Tibet singing bowl, and gentle yoga to maximize my oxygen intake. If there is a parking lot for shopping, I choose to park as far as possible to force myself to put in a few extra steps each day. Daily exercise has become my king, good nutrition my queen, and avoiding chemicals my prince, and I am living in a kingdom of determination to beat cancer.

Occasionally, my body would be subject to bacteria or viral infection because of my still-suppressed immune system. I avoid attending closed-door events packed full of people. Life could not be more tough than those COVID-19 days of lockdown and mask-wearing, but I still adopt the habit of wearing masks whenever I need to be at an indoor event or when taking a flight. My habit of carrying some hand sanitizer has stayed with me.

Casting my memory back to my daily physical therapy days during my treatment, there were days that I had to re-learn how to walk, how to squeeze a soft ball to regain my hand coordination and dexterity or walking my fingers against the wall to regain my shoulder's flexibility. Although I did not suffer from much nerve damage, I did have to re-learn a lot of basic bodily functions. The instruction manual for cancer does not exist, and the possible physical changes were not anticipated by me. I never predicted that my once-strong body could self-destruct at such a fast pace. On the other hand, I believe my body also learned how to recover as fast as it knew how to destroy itself.

As part of dealing with the physical changes, I had to develop my way of dealing with the loss of bodily functions. Apart from my faith, I had to seek additional ways for relaxation and spiritual sustenance. I also learned how to say no when my body could not cope. It was perfectly acceptable to take time away from people so I could sleep and rest. I remember the three days before my third chemotherapy, I sunk myself into the heavenly bed at the Westin Hotel and slept for three days straight. If my memory serves me well, Keith and Gigi were constantly seeking cold smoothies or ice cream to keep me hydrated since I was not able to eat solid food.

Chemotherapy wreaks havoc on the body. Since I was not able to be active or consume much food for three days, my blood work was a failure, with too much calcium. The doctor told me that Toby was extremely furious. When we arrived at the infusion center, my doctor put an emergency stop to my third chemotherapy. I was sent to emergency care instead. I had to spend forty-eight hours being infused to bring my calcium level to an acceptable level. Those forty-eight hours were a bewildering time, and I staggered around in great confusion. I cannot recall who took care of me because I was pretty much comatose most of the time.

When I woke up and saw a team of white-coated young and senior doctors forty-eight hours later, I realized that I was an exemplary patient who rebounded with great zest. The doctor who treated me was a professor, and he brought in a team of his student doctors to observe my recovery. It was like a scene from a Hollywood drama.

All I could see was a row of young doctors hovering over me as if I was an interesting object of study. It was amazing how the infusion helped me convalesce, and I requested three big steaks for breakfast. I remember the team of doctors smiling when they saw the amount of food I inhaled after my hibernation. I was compensating for missing a few days of dinners. It was amazing how my body wanted to heal, and there was a sense of euphoria when I awoke from the state of unconsciousness.

My red blood cells were somewhat below safety level, and I was admitted to the ER again for my very first blood transfusion. If I was a poet, I would have written a poem to those volunteers who donate their blood to save patients in need. I will never find out which donors' blood saved me, but I did pray hard and wished the donors a thousand years of good karma. Some people might object to receiving another person's blood, but I was not a fool because I knew if I did not accept the transfusion, I might not have a chance of defeating Toby.

I swiftly told my doctors to please sign me up. The medical teams do not take blood transfusions lightly, and the need for donor blood is assessed earnestly. To inject a bit of humor into that incident, I jokingly referred to my donor's blood as "a steak in the bag" to the nurses, and they liked it. I cannot quite recall how many "steaks in a bag" I had, but I do know that I carry a perpetual respect and appreciation for all blood donors. As I progressed to the remission state, I volunteered to donate my blood at the cancer center. However, my donation was not approved since my body still had some chemotherapy and radiation residue, and I was told that I needed to wait for a while before I could donate. I look forward to the day I may repay the blood I borrowed!

During the healing phase of recovery, I occasionally indulged myself in a bit of self-compassion. However, I limited the time I allowed myself to marinate in the pool of self-pity. In my experience, feeling sad for myself did not get me very far. As I mentioned previously, self-pity is not a healthy habit because it can be destructive and could have led me into a non-productive state of mind. There are a lot of chat groups for women with gynecological cancer who need to give each other a helping hand. Unless I was in need of information or I was in a positive mood to assist others, I aimed not to seek friendship among fellow cancer warriors. As most cancer comrades know, the cancer world is the worst place to meet good people. During the recovery phase of my journey, I could not afford to be constantly hearing about others' misery because gloomy outcomes saddened me. When I was told I was in remission, I certainly felt a tinge of guilt when I remembered those who did not make it.

The healing stage required major emotional intelligence to monitor how I felt. I was able to intelligently perceive others' complaints and suffering, and simultaneously, I was able to judiciously manage my emotions when I heard of bad news from others. All aspects of emotional perception, management, and utilization came to help me recover from my own trauma.

From the day of my remission, I seemed to have switched on a magic button in my mind that I would be freed and ceased to dwell in the past. Avoid self-pity at all costs because it can distort one's perception of cancer tragedy. I kept things in perspective and fought on as if the two years of battling Toby and Tory were just a slight diversion on my life's roadmap, and I am now back on the original track I had planned.

Apart from the physical side effects of cancer treatment, there was an annoying psychological deficiency in my recovery. I developed some social anxiety when it comes to dining out or eating with a big group of people. Food was tasteless during treatment, and food remained a threat to my mental well-being. During treatment, I was uneasy about eating a large meal because I had a fair number of traumatic memories caused by severe diarrhea and uncontrollable stomach cramps after consuming food. This unease with food is not cataclysmic, but I have worked hard to address it since I was able to admit I have an unhealthy relationship with food. When my world was spinning out of control with bouts of tough treatment, the only thing I felt that was within my sphere of influence was what I ate or did not eat. I am now able to write about this typically taboo topic with honesty, and without sugar-coating!

Chapter Twenty-Four

The Man Who Never Gave Up on Me

"I am the best thing that could ever happen to you. I am meant for you." – Josephine Spence

Our mindset is the baseline for our happiness. I certainly have become less materialistic and more focused on experiences. I believe everyone is entitled to seek happiness, but we must distinguish between pleasure and happiness. If I learned how to think like the Dalai Lama, I might just discover who I am, and be very contented with where I am. The ultimate goal for me is to ignore what I do not possess and stop eyeing my friends' bigger houses, newer cars, and better kitchens. I wish I knew how to be gratified with all Keith had sacrificed and provided to our marriage well before I fell ill.

I proposed to Keith in 1987. Yes, you heard right – I did propose to Keith when we completed our college degree during a walk along Earls Court Road in London. After three and a half years of dating, I was merely twenty-three years young and was unwilling to return to Malaysia after falling in love. I said to Keith, "Frankly, I am the best thing that could ever happen to you, and your mom told me I was the best thing that you dragged into her house."

With such a forceful proposal, I did not think Keith would reject me. He looked at me and said, "Okay. You pick a date, and I will show up."

Our wedding went ahead without my father or mother's approval. My parents were devastated and felt betrayed. They sent me to a boarding school in England for the best education but never expected me to marry a non-Asian man. Of course, I was saddened that I was the rule-breaker in the Loke family – the very first to be co-mingling with a man without a single drop of Chinese blood. My parents had hoped that I would be matched with some Malaysian doctor or well-to-do businessman. My marriage to Keith was considered a divergence from my traditional Chinese parents. It took many years before my dear papa accepted our marriage. Here we are, celebrating our thirty-six years of marriage, and we are still together.

There are some minor details I overlooked after proposing to Keith. As a Chinese daughter, it was a deadly crime not to obtain my parents' approval before the marriage. When I suggested the idea of marrying a non-Chinese English gentleman whom my parents had never met, it was as if I dropped a bombshell into the Loke family. My father was furious, and my mother was devastated. Never in the history of the Loke family had we admitted a single drop of non-Chinese blood. According to a hierarchical family structure, my next line of appeal was my eldest brother. So, in a very loving way, my eldest brother asked whether there was true love between myself and Keith. If so, I did have his full permission to proceed with the marriage. I am hence forever grateful to have such a decisive eldest brother, who took the brunt from my parents and ancestors. There will always be that extra respect I have for my eldest brother.

Keith is the organizer of all things in our family unit. Just before each holiday season, Keith would focus on acquiring gifts for his two girls, namely me and Gigi. He has a habit of collecting and engineering all sorts of gifts starting in July, well before December. As much as I love his total dedication to his two girls, I confessed to Keith that I never remembered what gifts were given to me every Christmas. What I did remember most were the things we did together, such as the very first time he held my hand on our first date in the city of London. As we crossed the busy streets, when the light turned green for pedestrians, Keith took the opportunity to hold my hand. Somehow, after we safely crossed the street, he never let my hand go. That was when the lightbulb came on for me, and I knew Keith's desire to hold my hand was equivalent to his asking me to be his girlfriend. I do not recall what Keith said to me that night, but I genuinely remember how he made me feel.

Every time Keith and I visit London, he ensures we return to the same spot where he first held my hand, i.e., outside of the Ritz Hotel London at 150 Piccadilly. After Gigi was born, we often walked past the Ritz when we visited London. Keith and I would always remind each other the exact intersection where he declared his undying love to me without uttering a word. This is just one of the million reasons I love my lifelong buddy, Keith; I place higher importance on how he holds my hands instead of what he buys for me. The vivid memories of our first time holding hands are pure bliss.

When we first relocated to Houston, the weather was starting to get hot. Somehow, Keith and I still wanted to treat our stay in Houston as though we were ordinary tourists. A short-term stay mentality was a cognitive necessity to tell me that my health issue was temporary.

We decided to take Gigi to visit the Houston Zoo as one did when there was a world-famous, well-kept zoo less than two miles from our rented apartment. It was a scorching Mother's Day in Houston. I had not yet started my treatment, and my pelvic area was bursting with pain. I could not walk, so Keith swiftly rented a wheelchair for me. The image of Keith pushing me in a wheelchair under the midday sun, drenched in sweat, reminded me of the couple, Max, and Bella (in a wheelchair) from the 1999 English romantic comedy *Notting Hill*. Notwithstanding any disagreement or argument Keith and I had ever had, I knew and remembered how this man loved me with or without cancer. The visit to the Houston Zoo felt just like the first time he held my hand and never let go. Being deeply loved by him gave me vigor as I felt secure in his arms. Knowing I had married the best husband on earth was pure elation.

During our stay in Houston, Keith made the extra effort of making our surroundings as normal as living in our own home. He cultivated the sense of homeliness by furnishing our bed with my own Egyptian cotton bedsheets, our pillows. Keith also furnished the kitchen with our own decorative items. Keith knew my happiness depended on my physical needs of living in a home instead of a hotel. One of my nephews airmailed three portraits of a cat, dog, and pig painted by his wife to our temporary abode. These portraits reminded me of all the animals we had at home. Humanizing and decorating our rented apartment fostered a sense of security. I would highly recommend this method of happiness cultivation for those who have to leave their familiar environment for a new city for treatment.

Being married to Keith for so many years, our relationship has been full of love and tenderness but often comes loaded with familiarity. The best way to elaborate on the role he plays in our relationship is to describe him as our catch-all kitchen drawer; he takes in all unidentifiable objects in our life without ever complaining. Miraculously, this well-worn-out drawer always gets cleaned out and reorganized without my knowledge. Keith takes on a lot of rubbish from me, and he subtly cleans up the mess without troubling me at all.

Our relationship is like a house. Whenever the light bulbs blow, we don't go and buy a new house; Keith just fixes the bulbs or whatever is causing the light bulbs to go off. Gigi and I look up to him, and we gave him the title, of Mr. Fix-It. Throughout my cancer treatment, I never had to worry about anything with our medical insurance. The fact that I had a man like Keith taking care of all things big or small so I might focus on fighting my battle with Toby was a crucial element to my swift recovery. Just like when Gigi was a toddler, whenever her toys broke, she would run around the house and told me to look for Mr. Fix-It.

During the recovery phase, I still had to have periodic blood work done at my local hospital. On the last visit, I saw an elderly man accompanied by his son. As they walked into the lobby of the infusion center, the son sadly told the nurse that his father would like his infusion line removed because his father no longer needed to continue with chemotherapy. I saw a hospital counselor approach the elderly man's son with a pamphlet for palliative care. Somehow, seeing the pain on this young man's face saddened me. Very often, removing the infusion line can be the celebratory event to mark the end of treatment because the medicine had sent the patient to remission, but in that situation, it was a case of no more treatment existing to save that elderly person. From the corner of my eyes, I saw tears rolling down his cheek while his father was taken by the nurse to disconnect his infusion line.

I teared up for that elderly patient inside my heart. I wanted so much to give his son a warm hug, but it was not permitted during COVID-19. Simultaneously, I prayed I would never have to let my beloved daughter and husband be handed a palliative care leaflet to read. Never did I wish my journey with Keith to entail such a deadly challenge, and I was most concerned about his caregiver burnout. Throughout the two years of cancer treatment, Keith demonstrated endless sympathy and compassion. God gave him the burden of caring for me, but sometimes, it seemed to me that God forgot to provide him with a shoulder to cry on. My beloved husband demonstrated his tenacity throughout my predicament from his effort to provide the security of good medical insurance to shopping for diapers to address my lack of bodily function control. Everything he did for me, be it big or small, he did with total, undying love. I did not have a choice of being paralyzed by my disease, but I certainly would choose to spend my whole life with this man who loves me unconditionally.

I remember Keith's jubilant face whenever I was able to eat food during my weakest days. He was most concerned about my weight loss, so he would search high and low for any nutritious food or drinks that I could handle. Whenever I could swallow ice cream or a mouthful of vitamin drinks, he would celebrate. There were nights when I had the sudden urge to have a mango ice cream, and he would jump out of the bed to go hunting in his pajamas.

I was scared of pain and often needed to numb it. At one point, I had the urge to consume alcohol to numb the body aches, so he would locate some alcoholic freeze pops knowing that I was almost a teetotaler. Somehow, the icy taste of alcoholic freeze pops for breakfast helped me to a good start on some days. The whole episode of cancer from being diagnosed to the stage of being cured was a symphony of pain and anguish. Throughout the suffering, I learned that pain had a purpose. Its intention was to teach me to slow down and to recalibrate my outlook in life. I also learned that even though Keith could not eliminate my pain, but he could take the edge off by being with me, holding my hands just like the very first time he held my hands outside of the Ritz in London.

Our rented apartment in Houston was conveniently located right next to the Intercontinental Hotel with a well-stocked kitchen and restaurant. When my taste buds were wrecked, I desired the most unusual food. Keith would line up all kinds of soup-based meals with the chef from the hotel next door just in case I fancied some. I was not an unreasonable patient to care for, but my erratic taste buds certainly gave Keith a lot of runarounds. This man loved me so even when I had no fight left in me.

Keith, thank you for never giving up on me.

Chapter Twenty-Five

Life Could Be Simple

*"Life is really simple, but we insist on making it complicated." –
Confucius*

I often ask myself, *is life simple, but we humans have made it complicated? Or is life so complicated, and we are just too simple to understand it?* I do not think I have a definitive answer to those questions, but I have started to lean towards living a much simpler lifestyle after becoming a patient.

To release my inner peace, I needed to be free of any unwanted possessions that might have inadvertently burdened me in my pre-cancerous days. I started to declutter my worldly goods with the knowledge that I would not have a U-Haul behind my hearse. The very first thing I did was clear out my work clothes, which I no longer needed, and donated them to my local charity shop. They took up space in my walk-in closet, which prevented me from actually walking into it. They also collected a lot of white specks of dust around the shoulders of the designer jackets.

I had a collection of recyclable plastic containers which could benefit others. One sunny day, I decided to ruthlessly pack up all my designer work clothes in those plastic containers and bid farewell to them. To quote Marie Kondo, "Never discard anything without saying thank you or goodbye." I said my sincere thank you to them and let them be recycled in my local charitable organizations. Those work clothes gave me the ability to dress well and professionally during my heyday, and they did spark joy but were no longer required in my simpler life.

I often choose to wake up to music, be it Bach's "Cello Suite in G Major" or Snoop Dog's "Gin and Juice." I let my morning mood decide my choice each day. The broad range of my music preferences often surprise my family and friends. Like an entry on a movie soundtrack, Keith knew exactly what scene he'd be confronted with just by listening to my playlist.

Some mornings, we had the intense scenes of *Jaws,* and some days we had the undemanding scenes of *Lawrence of Arabia*'s desert ride on his camels. Between Keith and I, we have unspoken words to forewarn each other how we're feeling each day, and this approach has been the secret ingredient to our almost forty-year relationship.

Nowadays, perhaps because of my lack of stress, I have lost the ability to perspire. Some would argue that the amount of radiation I received has led to a medical condition known as hypohidrosis or anhidrosis, which I believe a certain royal prince is familiar with. I seem to have literally and physically taken the "don't sweat the small stuff" approach seriously.

I first noticed my lack of sweat when I visited my mother in the tropical countries of Singapore and Malaysia. While others were begging for air conditioners, I was asking for another sweater. On the hot summer days in Houston, others were wearing thin T-shirts while I was covering myself with woolly beanies and thick jackets, which I brought with me from Chicago. Playing pickleball with my neighbors, I wore a thick turtleneck and was unable to produce a single drop of sweat while my opponents were drenched. After three hours of Zumba, I was still not clammy while fellow dancers were dripping like a sprinkler.

With my medical team's permission, I continued my recovery with a sauna and steam room regimen in an effort to encourage my body to reacquaint itself with perspiring. My simple life needs daily meditation with the serene sounds of spa-like running water and thunderstorms. This is how I detox physically and mentally for a gentle start each morning. The six o'clock alarms are no longer welcome in my tranquil and unruffled bedroom. I believe that I have simplified my morning routines to facilitate a gentler way of waking up.

I am not much of a farmer, but I have become an enthusiastic producer of organic and homegrown vegetables. We have a patch on our property that gets unlimited sunshine during sunny days. This patch was converted into a vegetable garden as a wedding anniversary gift from Keith to me. Magically, I have been able to produce strawberries, cucumbers, tomatoes, cabbages, rhubarb, zucchinis, and eggplants, to name a few.

Among our neighbors, we have an arrangement with elderly horticulturist Mr. Hanson, who is the most well-informed grower of all things organic. Every spring day, Mr. Hanson collects the horse manure for his acres of vegetable garden. In exchange, I receive an unlimited supply of organic vegetables from him.

Likewise, with my excess production of tomatoes, my neighbors, Bettie, and Charlie, reward me with their organic eggs. With this simple life, I have become a true organic consumer free of pesticides. The camaraderie of comparing each other's fruit and vegetables every spring and summer has become a highlight of my new simpler but more contented life.

I have been very blessed to own horses who have been my faithful companions since my twenties. Horses are very much a part of our family life. Given the limitations of my blood thinners, I am still unable to ride like a wild cowboy for the time being. However, I choose to spend my spare time with these furry four-legged children. The mere act of feeding hay and grooming them are a joy and stress-reliever. There are days I could roll in the pastures with my two geldings and make snow angels together. The love between my horses and I is implicit, and we all know not to hurt one another while we roll together. The world becomes at peace when there is no one around to judge our silly acts.

Chapter Twenty-Six

No Stone Unturned When It's All Over

"*D*on't *try to understand life. Live it.*" – *Osho*

When cancer hit me, I had a wake-up call. Life became an ocean of unknowns and unfinished business. I wanted to live life with gusto and to ensure I left no stone unturned in case life became short. Someone once said, "Life is a great big canvas, and you should throw all the paint on it you can."

Yesterday marked the end of Dr. Karen's fight with Chucky. Chucky had tortured her to no end and assaulted her lungs, brain, and most major organs in between. Her cancer originated from her ovaries. Dr. Karen was a beautiful young individual who received her diagnosis on the same day as me. Admittedly, her departure last night clouded my head with immense despondency.

Today, I woke up six feet above the ground but felt sad for all those who were snatched away by this repugnant and spiteful disease. I decided I needed to revisit my so-called bucket list. I want to ensure I utilize the time I have with no remorse nor sorrow. That is to say, I will finish whatever I have not yet finished and exorcise whatever ill feelings I ever had with an aim for a perfect use of my precious time.

I was offered a financially sound opportunity to return to work, but I politely rejected the offer simply because my rebirth apprised me that searching for the previous version of me would only lead to disappointment. It is high time that I splashed all the colors there are on my canvas.

One of the things Keith and I plan to do is walk in front of the Ritz London just like the very first time he held my hand some forty years ago, listening to the sound of the nightingale, which sang in Berkeley Square (but pronounced as Barkley) in London. We wanted to repeat our dating days when we both were students in the swinging London scenes of the 80s. To repeat the little things we did, such as eating fish and chips with tons of vinegar wrapped in newspaper after coming out of class on cold winter days. I might even go as far as eating a pickled onion from the yellowy mason jars in the fish and chip shop just for the sake of nostalgia.

Visiting one of London's markets in search of freshly fried donuts might even make it on my bucket list. Nightclubbing on a poor student budget was not frequent, but Keith did work to save money to take me out occasionally. Forty years after dating, he still often talks about the tiny red dress I wore when we danced the night away to the *Saturday Night Fever* hits. However, I know Keith wants his Cornish pasties and English pork pies as his priority when we return to London's notorious bakeries.

The month before removing my chemotherapy port, we decided to take a flight to London, and Gigi joined us from New York in time for the coronation of King Charles III. We revisited our dating spots and took in a few shows at the West End theatres. We checked off a few items on my bucket list, but importantly, Keith and I re-walked the path near the Ritz London, and he held my hand to cross the street just like he did some forty years ago. I fell in love with him all over again.

Since we often go back to London to connect with family, we frequently stay in the Grosvenor House Hotel, which is quiet but very centrally located. I recall that during holiday season, it is just like a scene out of a Charles Dickens novel: men dressed in dark winter coats roasting winter chestnuts near the foyer of the hotel. The aroma of roasted chestnuts just outside lingers in my nose for a long time. It reminds me of when Keith and I brought Gigi and Keith's mother to the Opera House in Covent Garden for a ballet show. Gigi had been a little child who wore a dark blue Harrods woolly coat that was two sizes too big, and we had a classic London scene of Gigi holding her beloved grandmother's hand in a black cab. Grandma Joan always had a plastic cover on her well-kept hair when it rained (which was a lot of the time). London is the place Keith and I met, and London will always hold a special spot in my heart.

I always wanted to find a life that was well worth living and be able to confront adversity with nonconformist hope and courage. Whoever said that fighting cancer isn't hard must have been deceitful. I fought each day for survivorship like John McEnroe in his fifth set at Wimbledon. The main goal was not to give up and be that ray of light for all those who were living in the darkness of cancer. Getting to the fifth set was tough enough, but having the determination to win the match was an even more crucial mindset for a cancer winner.

After winning the fifth set of the match, I wanted to live life as if there is no heaven after death by manifesting my own version of paradise on earth. Very often I do not give a flying fudge about other people's opinions or gossip. I shall live my truth and continue to pursue my own bliss. To be truthful, Toby did not make me a survivor because I always was. If anything, Toby gave me the urgency to enjoy life. He also taught me it is okay to fall apart sometimes, and to lose my Wonder Woman cape in times of fear is acceptable. I also learned that I do not have to be the leader all the time and being in control is just an illusion. By staying still on the chemotherapy chair and the radiation bed, I learned to let others take the wheel for a change.

Chapter Twenty-Seven

Be Kind to Your Caregivers and Yourself

"I can't be anything to anyone if I am nothing to myself." – Alex Elle

In my earlier chapters, I mentioned that a cancer patient's emotions can be complicated and difficult to explain. There are so many reasons to become bitter when you are diagnosed with cancer. On this road of suffering, it is okay to be lost or sometimes temporarily unsure of your position. If you are a cancer survivor, do not feel guilty. If you are still battling the disease, please remember there is a purpose because we were chosen.

Today was the day I met a wonderful and intelligent girlfriend, Dr. Cerise, who lived through the cancer journey with her mother, and she began to articulate how badly she was treated while being a caregiver.

Dr. Cerise was the only daughter in the family, and she became the de facto caregiver when cancer inundated her mother. Through the stress of daily care, her mother began to use her as a punching bag. The verbal abuse and outpouring of anger onto her daughter broke Dr. Cerise's heart. Even after years of healing, she still got a lump in her throat when she recalled those tough years. Her mother survived the ordeal, but it took nearly eighteen years to repair their relationship.

It is often said that cancer fighters are mere passive recipients of the disease, and not being in control can distort our personality. However, I cannot fathom how a cancer patient can become abusive and un-mannerly to the loved ones who sacrifice their precious time to provide daily care. I often instructed Keith to remind me, "Don't be an ass," should I become an obnoxious patient.

In writing this chapter, my intent is not to marginalize the emo-tional complexity of a cancer patient but to remind my fellow cancer warriors that sometimes the disease is harder for the caregivers to process than the patients themselves. Receiving a cancer diagnosis was the most fear-provoking experience I've ever had. I often felt lonely, but I also reminded myself that my bucket was half-full and never half-empty. I had a choice to see joyfulness and feel blessed. I found joy even in the tiniest things that made me feel alive, no matter how Toby and Tory forced me out of my comfort zone. By being joyful, happiness inevitably got allotted to the people surrounding me.

To genuinely enjoy my life, I became grateful for things we often take for granted: being able to breathe, walk, swallow my food, and retain control of bodily functions. Being able to use the restroom in a timely manner without soiling myself, as fundamental as it was, seemed a major form of achievement during my darkest days. Those were the basic things that Toby and Tory attempted to deprive me of.

What I longed for was Keith's understanding when I did not have any bodily functions due to the treatment. I no longer longed for Hallmark cards or flowers from my loved ones. The mere ability to hold their hands while the excruciating pain endeavored to terminate me was more than adequate. Although I was not a saint, I truly never attempted to expose my frustrations to my loved ones. Whenever I asked for some reflection to ascertain whether I became an ass during our painful journey, the only thing he could mention was my unpredictable eating habits and the lack of passion for food, which caused him to be anxious. Maybe he was being kind by claiming that he had erased all the bad memories.

One of my fellow cancer warriors, Catherine, was a young mother with a four-year-old daughter. She would often tell me how she yelled at her daughter when the pain got intolerable. After her unreasonable loss of temper with her young child, she would lock herself in a room and post her tears of regrets on social media. Catherine was crying out for help. I would often find myself tongue-tied when I knew the hardship Catherine was experiencing. From the patient's perspective, I sympathized with her pain because cancer pains are the most incommunicable agonies. The whole body would hurt from the head to the tiny end of our toes.

The fact that Catherine lost her temper with a young child could not be excused, but I could only attribute it to her pain. I believe some people had their mother as their first love. From the moment I set eyes on my newborn to the day I cheered Gigi for walking across the Radio City stage to receive her undergraduate degree. I knew there is not a word accurate enough to encapsulate the bond between a mother and her child. I was proud of how Gigi handled my sickness. She was poised and pragmatic about the whole ordeal and very often contributed to the family with logical solutions to help me cope.

The days when I was allowed home back in Illinois, Gigi would take me to the medical marijuana stores (since it was then legal in Illinois) to procure some natural painkillers. Gigi knew I could not tolerate opioids for pain, and she also knew I was dead set against taking marijuana, even medical marijuana. Somehow, our mother-daughter bond was further enriched when Gigi drove me to a dispensary blasting Snoop Dog. I felt loved by my daughter, who was a college senior. Somehow, we were not mortified at all and swaggered into a dispensary as a mother and daughter team. Whenever the pain got too much, we would have our bonding over a pack of medicated gummy bears. I did not become a drug addict from the opioids or marijuana extracts; I merely became an understanding mother. When possible and legal, turning to natural painkillers did save me from becoming an impossible parent to care for. I always believed I was chosen to have cancer to bring me closer to my daughter.

No cancer patient can turn back the clock to invent a new beginning, but for sure, we can make the best of our predicament to conjure a brand-new ending. To my fellow cancer fighters, if your days are bad, please remember not to become an ass to your loved ones. Remember that your children, husband, wife, partner, dog or even your goldfish did not cause your cancer. Hearts are breakable and even though time can lessen the intensity of painful memories, time cannot remove the scars. If you remember some of your behaviors might have hurt your caregivers, pick up the phone or write a nice apology note to the one you hurt while you were not yourself. Tomorrow is never guaranteed, and we all need to mend our broken bridges before time runs out. Do not allow the disease to mean more than your personal relationships with your family and friends.

In certain parts of my cancer voyage, I started to blame myself for becoming cancerous. I talked about how to avoid being abusive to your loved ones and to never try to use your children as your emotional crutches. In this chapter, I also wanted to cover the topic of self-care and self-love for a cancer patient. Not every patient needs to behave like a saint while wrestling with this spiteful disease. However, we can live life with a fresh start.

I started taking yoga lessons to educate myself on how to relax and meditate. Sure enough, I have not mastered the Three-Legged Dog or the Pigeon positions. My Pigeon pose looks more like a rotisserie chicken on a skewer, but who is there to judge? Nobody.

While Keith is no Fred Astaire, we have taken up ballroom dancing, and I happily play Ginger Rogers in his loving arms. I also took up Zumba classes even though I was born with two left feet and can barely coordinate my limbs, but I show up for my classes each week and declared to the trainer that I would dance like no one is watching. I dance to the familiar hip-hop music as if I had torn off the bandages on my chemotherapy port. In addition, I Zumba as if I am not sober.

Being kind to oneself is the best way to live during cancer recovery. I have acquired a shower radio which allows me to sing and dance to the beat of my own drums. No one can tell me my singing is out of tune in a shower. I learned rules were made to be broken, and we all should laugh and dance in the face of adversity. Sing out of tune or use the wrong lyrics even if it is annoying for the people who cohabit with you. Don't ever doubt your self-worth. Every shower you stop singing would be a shower wasted.

It is high time to celebrate us as cancer winners, and I have come to a complete stop as my own critic in everything I do. After all, the person I am with most of my life is myself, so learn to love yourself deeply and devotedly. As I have been able to love myself and everything I do, I have discovered respect, authenticity, and fulfillment.

I enjoy meditation with the Tibet singing bowl gifted by my dear girlfriend. The simple act of circling my fingers around the rim presents me with clarity. Most of this book was formulated during my meditation and quiet walks in my village. I learned that even the bluest sky can be obscured by the occasional cloud. Once the clouds move, I probably would not remember what cloudiness looked like.

Beautiful people come through stormy weather. I learned what defeat tastes like. I learned the meaning of pain, struggling, and hurt. I also know what it feels like to be freed from chemotherapy and radiation. I have acquired the ability to empathize with others' suffering, be they small or big.

During those challenging times, I never looked to Keith to fix me nor Gigi to cheer me up. If I ever was getting annoyed with myself and attempted to slam my frustration on my caregivers, I would swiftly remind myself the very moment when Keith held my hand on our first date. The romantic lights from the Ritz London will always remind me that he was the one who held my hand first; therefore, he must have loved me maybe one and a half minute longer than I have loved him. I could confess that I was so dazed during my treatment that I could not have lost my temper with Gigi due to my lack of energy. However, I would always remind myself how she flew back and forth from New York to Houston to cheer me up.

There is no such thing as a perfect relationship, but a near-perfect one is the relationship that all parties work on to make perfect. When I was in the cancer storm, I knew I always had Keith, Gigi, and my siblings, and they were always ready and waiting to shelter me with their umbrella of love. Today, my health is in a much steadier state. Between now and death, I would very much like to hold my umbrella to safeguard them in return.

Chapter Twenty-Eight

My Rearview Mirror

"*You can learn to be happy in any circumstances.*" – *Robert Louis Stevenson*

I was not a religious person before my adventure with Toby and Tory, but I became a Jesus-loving and happiness-seeking Dalai Lama admirer. Short of wearing the yellow saffron robe, I did embrace my bald-headedness and studied the art of meditation. I learned that we all have the right to pursue unbridled happiness in life. I wanted to take up daily journaling, but I could not put pen to paper until I had a fair idea of how my story would end. My beloved sister even bought me a vintage desk nicely situated in the quietest part of my house to enable my writing, since she knew I had been a creative storyteller ever since I was a little kid.

As a young girl in elementary school, I was so creative and frequently authored weekly stories and articles for our hometown newspaper.

The joy of being able to use an anonymous writer's name and collecting one Malaysian ringgit per article was the pride of my early years. I had worked hard and collected an adequate number of ringgits to acquire a little bicycle, which my dear daddy did not approve of since he was of the opinion that bicycles were not meant for ladies. The bicycle was my ticket to date since most young boys and girls looked for privacy in quiet parks and I was no exception. My bilingual education allowed me to write in Chinese fluently for our local paper, and I remained anonymous as I contributed to the publication for many years under my fake name.

When I went to a Catholic convent school in England, I was encouraged by my English teacher to write in English. When I was a teenager, I was once publicly humiliated by a member of my family that my writing would never amount to anything major since English was not my first language. The humiliation prompted me to put away my authoring pen. Looking back, I should not have let that incident extinguish my love for writing, whether in Chinese or English.

At the beginning of this book, I described myself as a polychronic high-flying and career-minded executive at home and in my work life. Given my diagnosis was that I might have been facing death twenty months ago, I dropped all things stressful, which required me to dash through my days with high productivity. Trivial things no longer unsettle me. I wrote this book and was true to myself, and I became ever so slightly humbled by the hard knocks of the disease. I began to question my purpose in life: was my life goal to be wealthy or to be healthy? Seeking happiness was not a self-centered act or a skillset that came pre-loaded in our DNA the day we were born. Being able to grasp happiness is a life skill. I began to re-align my mindset on what made me fulfilled.

The horrible disease of cancer did not come with an instruction manual, especially the physiological and emotional aspects. If I went into battle against Toby and Tory believing the treatment was a lost cause, I would not have survived, and this book would not have been written. I thank my inner strength and survivor instincts, which served me well. I also realize if there was no winter to freeze my tail off in Chicago, I would not have been able to appreciate the warmth of spring and summer. If I did not have the task of battling Toby and Tory, I would not have learned to be compassionate to others who have suffered. The school of cancer occasionally brought me down to my knees, and it was meant to be, because being down and nearly out made me appreciate the power of prayer.

An individual's inner strength emanates from their outlook on life and the belief that happiness can be found. Overall, I believe the fundamental premise in life is to seek happiness. Once happiness has been found, it should be reciprocated to the people around you. Many life coaches and psychologists talked about self-actualization, fulfillment, self-esteem, and life satisfaction, among other capacious words. I found the simpler definition of happiness is, the easier happiness can be ascertained.

My body might be wounded and bruised, but it will regain its strength. When adversity happens in life, it only means some great things are sure to follow.

This week, I had my chemotherapy port surgically removed at MD Anderson. This is a major milestone since the unplugging of the once-very-useful chemotherapy port signifies my divorce from cancer. Therefore, it makes total sense for me to cease writing about my cancer voyage from now on. The scars from my chemotherapy port and my IVC will not fade. They are the mark of a victor and a badge of honor. I will always wear my scars with pride.

After the cancer storm clouds lifted, life became sweeter than ever. I shall continue to make my positive mindset contagious to those who are going through treatment. I will never give up the fight to extend my life because it is worthwhile.

To conclude this book, I would like to share my view on surviving in the ocean of cancer: "Once a river flows into the cancer sea, expect stormy wind and rain flying in sideways. Do not pray to God for the rain to stop, but merely ask God for a bigger and stronger umbrella!"

Epilogue

To my daughter,

One day, should you miss me and cannot find me, please do not worry. You will find the U-Haul containing all my belongings, the rocks I accumulated, the trees I planted, the secret recipe to my rice surprise, the smell of my burned cooking, the sound of my out-of-tune singing, the fingerprints when I first held your hands. Most importantly, you will find the dust on the books I authored. My fortitude to fight for survivorship shall live on and on!

You will always be the butterfly in my stomach, the Yo-Yo Ma to my cello, my "Haiyaa" to my Uncle Roger, and the aria in my opera. I love you endlessly.

About the Author

Josephine Spence is a daughter, wife, and mother. She is a seasoned consultant and CEO in the information technology arena before she embarked on her cancer adventure. Dr. Spence used to write for her hometown newspaper as a young child in Chinese but stopped writing for a long time. Apart from her dissertation on emotional intelligence and workplace resistance to change, this is Dr. Spence's first book, and she is inspired by everything she learned during her cancer odyssey. Writing has been a form of self-therapy during her recovery, and Dr. Spence hopes this book reaches those who are struggling in the darkness of cancer.

Dr. Spence was born in Malaysia and educated in the United Kingdom but now lives with her husband, daughter, horses, and cats on a small farm in Illinois, USA.